A Production Handboo.

A Production Handbook

A guide to the pitfalls of programme making

Peter Jarvis

Focal Press
An imprint of Butterworth-Heinemann Ltd
Linacre House, Jordan Hill, Oxford OX2 8DP

A member of the Reed Elsevier group

OXFORD LONDON BOSTON
MUNICH NEW DELHI SINGAPORE SYDNEY
TOKYO TORONTO WELLINGTON

First published in 1993

British Library Cataloguing in Publication Data
A catalogue record for this book is available from the British Library

ISBN 0 240 51344 4

Library of Congress Cataloguing in Publication Data
A catalogue record for this book is available from the Library of Congress

Photoset by Deltatype Ltd, Ellesmere Port, Cheshire
Printed and bound in Great Britain by Redwood Books, Trowbridge, Wiltshire

Contents

Preface

A successful television production is a cocktail of perspiration, inspiration, and organization.

The perspiration becomes evident the moment the beginner discovers that television is not very glamorous and that every programme is hemmed in by deadlines and budget constraints imposed by producers, commissioning editors, clients, or sponsors. The inspiration should be taken for granted. If you don't feel sure that you have a talent, and if the hard work isn't always rewarding and fun, then you are in the wrong game. Whether you are planning a meteoric career in 'the media' or simply hoping to progress from home videos to shooting weddings and bar mitzvahs you need a vital creative spark which no book can ever give you. However, the creative aspect can be over rated. I have squirmed through many awful college, film or video showings which have demonstrated what can happen when TV is treated as high art without proper attention to basic production crafts.

There are shelves of books analysing classic productions frame by frame or delving into screenplays word by word which illuminate points of ideology, semiology, de-constructionism or the significance of deep focus photography. I do not intend to add to their numbers. This book is about the third ingredient, the 'boring bit' that is fobbed off on PAs and Production Managers in big companies or too often put aside by newcomers to small ones. That is, organization.

The first law of programme making is 'Murphy's Law' also known as 'Sod's Law'. If anything can go wrong it will. Things go wrong too often for beginners because without experience it is difficult to spot trouble coming and take the necessary steps to head it off. Traditionally, in both the film and television industries one used to learn one's craft like an apprentice, by progressing from humble to more and more ambitious projects, and by absorbing the wisdom and experience of colleagues. Producers and directors learnt their trades at the not always gentle hands of film editors and cameramen, as well as from established and distinguished figures in their own areas of the business. What they could and could not get away with in matters of law, copyright or taste was drummed into them by editors and departmental heads, as well as wise and experienced PAs. But the 1980s saw a transformation in the industry, amounting to a revolution which has not yet run its course.

These changes were due to political and social and economic factors as well as the introduction of new technology.

It is only a short time since Channel 4 spawned a regiment of new production companies, independent of the BBC and ITV broadcasting duopoly. Now the giants themselves have opened up their wavelengths to a 25% share for independents and there is every reason to think that this proportion will increase. Some of the new ITV franchise holders are effectively becoming publishers of programmes rather than programme makers. Satellite television is upon us, cable television production waits hopefully in the wings, and a fifth national channel is promised. However at the time of writing there seems no clear idea of how the increased air time will be filled. With such a rapid expansion it's difficult to remember that breakfast and daytime television, and programming after midnight are all recent developments in Britain. The rise of the domestic video recorder from being an expensive toy in a range of competing formats to its current status as a universal piece of household equipment has also been a significant development.

To date most of these new developments have been serviced by production and technical staff who won their spurs, or at least got a basic training, from the BBC or one of the ITV companies. But as the independent franchise holders perceptibly move in the direction of becoming publishers, and as the BBC retrenches (or crumbles, according to your point of view) the programme makers will have to emerge from somewhere else.

There is above all an accelerating spread of television outside the heartland of broadcasting. Corporate productions, music videos, instructional and training programmes, promotional tapes, tele-conferencing, multi-media, videotape publishing and so on have opened up new sectors into which are rushing an army of people who have had no contact with the traditions of the established broadcast companies. And every year the available technical equipment gets cheaper, and more sophisticated, and more user friendly. The old mystique is gone when anyone with a few pounds to spare can go to a local shopping centre to buy a camcorder as good as the most sophisticated professional equipment of fifteen years ago.

It is for these newcomers, whether students of the media, hopeful amateurs, or recent converts from journalism, publicity and the audio-visual world, that this guide is intended.

Life in the big broadcasting organizations was wonderfully sheltered. Managing budgets was a standardized procedure. Specialist departments dealt with contracts, copyright, union agreements and insurance. A lawyer was on call when trouble threatened, a shipping agent would smooth the way to foreign adventures, and a safety officer struggled to restrain the more homicidal inclinations of directors. Above all there was the continuous, hardly noticed back-up of experienced producers, engineers, librarians, designers, PAs and dozens more, to offer advice and steer the beginner round the likely consequences of folly or ignorance.

In our new world it ain't necessarily so.

As far as I know this is the first book which takes Murphy's Law as its theme and concentrates on what pitfalls a programme maker *ought to avoid*.

Any attempt to bring together subjects as diverse as the qualifications of stuntmen and the Rehabilitation of Offenders Act is not likely to achieve an encyclopaedic list of every known pitfall. One of the joys and terrors of programme making is that every new project throws up new problems and new challenges. The goalposts keep moving. Copyright law has only just been completely overhauled, new legislation on freedom of information, and the protection of privacy may be around the corner. Harmonization with the laws and procedures of the other EEC countries is now only really beginning to make its impact.

In such circumstances this book cannot attempt to be a definitive work. I must take the blame for any errors of fact or tendentious opinions. I have no reason to doubt that Murphy's Law afflicts those who write about television any less than those who make it.

This is no more than a guide. You have a better chance of avoiding trouble if you are aware of the directions from which problems are likely to come.

I hope that readers of this book will, in the future, avoid hearing the famous Laurel and Hardy line, 'This is another fine mess you've gotten us into!'

Peter Jarvis

CHAPTER 1

On location

Barney Oldfields Race for Life, pre-1914. Still provided by the British Film Institute.

Public places

One ponderous legal joke is that it is impossible to venture on the public highway without risking arrest. If you run you may be causing a disturbance, if you stop you may be causing an obstruction, and if you stroll slowly you may be loitering with intent. Of course the moment you fall in with the company of others the list becomes truly wonderful and the possibilities range through begging or soliciting to riotous assembly.

Now you might spend a lifetime as an honest citizen about his business without getting into any such trouble with the law. But as a member of a location crew you are very likely to find that the lawyers' joke is based on serious realities.

The crew and the police

If you are trying to get anything more ambitious than a few hand-held shots always notify the local police station what you are up to, where you intend to be and when. Although in some relaxed parts of the country the local Duty Sergeant may wave you on with amusement or indifference it is more than a common courtesy to write or at the least make a telephone call outlining your plans.

In the London Metropolitan Area for example, failure to notify the police of your intentions with specific location details and times may lead to the crew being moved on, or held up whilst their credentials are checked.

Location crews can be pests to the local community. Camera crews attract crowds. A tripod on a pavement can be an obstruction for pedestrians. Camera cars can block traffic when they are being used for tracking shots and in-car interviews or illegally park when they are stationary for the loading and unloading of gear. Directors and reporters can offend proprietors and customers by blocking shop entrances, recordists may demand that workmen silence noisy machines and switch off their transistors, cameramen may order members of the public not to walk through shot leaving them with the choice of hanging about during a take or stepping off the kerb and under a bus.

There are several other good reasons for not acting in a cavalier manner with the police.

There are a few places, and many public events, where you will need official press accreditation, so don't hope to be able to drop in for a few shots of Downing Street or elbow your way onto a television stand for your own interpretation of the Trooping of the Colour. Crews should always carry some sort of official identification, if not a press card. The police are unlikely to forbid you to film under normal circumstances although they may impose conditions such as not allowing tripods on busy thoroughfares or vetoing camera cars.

On the other hand they may agree to turn a blind eye to local parking regulations for you, although if this necessitates suspending metre bays you may have to pay the local authority.

Never forget that a television camera acts like a magnet for some people. Beggars and alcoholics have long since learned to pester and intimidate crews as a sure way to extort large sums to go away. Some teenagers can't resist leaping in front of the lens to wave, shout and make obscene gestures. In some areas there are minorities who associate the cameras with police surveillance. I've even been verbally abused by umbrella-waving citizens while making bucolic short videos about a London park. It appeared that I was personally responsible for screen nudity and the increase in the television licence fee!

All this adds up to the fact that it is by no means uncommon for a crew to need the help of a passing policeman and you are likely to get scant cooperation if he wasn't notified of your presence at the outset.

Security

Since crews seem to have become increasingly prone to random violence and obstruction a number of security firms have set up sections of private show guards to act as minders and to protect cars and equipment. An estate car loaded with shiny aluminium boxes is such an obvious target for car thieves that many cameramen insist on one crew member always remaining behind. But if you need and can afford show guards, check the credentials of the available firms and try to get a personal recommendation from another customer.

A leading broadcast company was embarrassed when one of its own hired security men was arrested for carrying concealed weapons at the Notting Hill Carnival.

Private Property

To reduce the effects of outside interference restrict your shoot as far as possible to private property. Much more property is private than first meets the eye. Most public parks and spaces are in effect private but you need to obtain permission, and frequently pay a fee, to use them.

No. 833

METROPOLITAN POLICE

FILMING IN STREETS

The following notes are issued for the information and guidance of persons undertaking filming in the streets and public places:-

(1) Nothing in the nature of a staged crime or street disturbance will be permitted.

(2) No filming can be permitted which would interfere with the operation of the parking meter schemes or give rise to any contravention of Road Traffic Acts or Regulations.

(3) Any filming must be undertaken on the sole responsibility of the promoters and participants, and no facilities can be granted by Police.

(4) The Commissioner of Police has no power to authorize the use of streets for the purposes of filming and does not issue permits purporting to do so, but police will not normally object to proposed filming provided that:-

(a) No obstruction or annoyance is caused and the directions of police on duty are observed.

(b) In the event of complaints being made or annoyance being caused filming ceases immediately at the request of Police.

(c) Where artificial lighting is used care must be taken to ensure that no obstruction or danger is caused by cables, wires, etc., and no danger or annoyance is caused by dazzle from the lights.

(d) As far as possible filming is arranged to take place when traffic, both vehicular and pedestrian, is lightest, e.g., on a Sunday morning.

(e) When it is proposed to film actors dressed in police uniforms, rehearsals are to be carried out in plain clothes. The fitting of gongs, bells, two-tone horns and blue flashing lights to pseudo-police vehicles is prohibited by law.

(f) Any special requirements of police about a particular filming are observed.

M.P.72(E)

Trafalgar Square is a private place, so you will need permission to shoot there.

Of course some crews can and do get away with not obtaining formal permission or paying a fee but the risks are high. The longer and more complex your scene, the greater the chance of being found out and it will cost you a lot in time and money to reshoot the scene elsewhere.

Shopping precincts and markets

Increasingly shopping precincts and malls are privately owned and privately policed by security companies who keep their areas permanently surveilled by their own cameras and whose job is to expel undesireables, apprehend thieves, and jump on unauthorized non fee-paying television crews. Even old fashioned open air markets often take place on private land and shooting is only permitted after negotiations with the market inspectors or firm of auctioneers. City markets frequently have a fixed scale of fees for productions. In some cases there is a flexibility based on an eye for the commercial main chance, i.e. a visiting foreign feature film unit may pay through the nose, but if you represent the local college you may get the fee waived, so long as you ask first.

In much used and abused locations like London's Covent Garden the Inspectors book crews by the hour both for financial and logistical reasons – too many lights and cameras littering the place on a given day can mean a loss of income for the traders. The steady replacement of film by video has at least done away with the two competing crews at Covent Garden wrecking each others scenes with rattling clapper boards and howls of 'Action' and 'Cut'.

Parks

Public parks are much the same. Most urban authorities reserve the right to charge for using their land for location purposes. Local bureaucrats can be sticklers for formality and whilst one may wave you on for the effort of a telephone call another might insist on a written request and a wait for approval from a town hall executive. Things can change. One west London Park had a well known procedure whereby producers would arrive at a park office at opening time, pay a nominal cash fee, and get a day pass. Then visiting crews started circumventing the formality or even bouncing cheques. Lately one of the most pleasant locations for miles is available only after a Kafkaesque exchange of formalities.

Recently some local authorities, including some London Boroughs, have set up film offices to coordinate the various departmental permissions, and some cities such as Liverpool and Birmingham have established film commissions. The primary aim of these commissions is to encourage feature film companies, particularly foreign ones, to spend their money and not be driven elsewhere by problems of transport, accommodation and bureaucracy.

Some Parks, like London's Royal Parks, are administered by the Department of the Environment which has its own police patrols. Obtaining permission to use Royal Parks is only grudgingly given and it can be a time-consuming procedure. You are most likely to be admitted if your subject is a documentary about the park itself; you are least likely to be admitted if you hope to use the location for a commercial or as a setting for any dramatized action.

Generally the nearer you get to Hyde Park Corner from any part of the UK the more likely you are to get into bureaucratic and security problems. But the problems are not exclusively metropolitan.

MoD properties

Ministry of Defence properties are subject to special procedures. This includes obvious locations like dockyards and whole swathes of English countryside used by the military including large parts of Dorset, Wiltshire, Norfolk and Wales.

Railways

The railways are subject to their own safety regulations and by-laws. British Rail has its own Transport Police and crews must usually be accompanied at all times on railway property. Underground railway systems are subject to particularly stringent regulations for obvious safety reasons so never hope to turn up at your local underground station for a quick word with disgruntled passengers. You will not be allowed to cross the forecourt.

Public bodies

That is the bad news. The good news is that under the 'enterprise culture' encouraged by Government during the 1980s all sorts of public bodies have been obliged to look to ways to generate income and some which once looked down their noses at production companies now roll out the red carpet. Stately homes, famous schools, hospitals, and even graveyards are available. But beware, everyone is looking for a profitable deal. For example if you want to shoot in Oxford, even for the simplest documentary purposes, the use of any likely location owned by either the colleges or the City Council at the time of writing will cost you a minimum of £150 to £200 per hour.

Commercial properties

So maybe the answer is to find some commercial or private property where no officialdom can interfere. Permission to film in a shopping mall or market does not of course include permission to operate in any particular premises. Some shops protest even when you try to shoot in front of their window displays. Generally small owner-run shops are easiest. Either they will be delighted or tell you to get lost. Larger enterprises like supermarkets and branches of chain stores frequently employ press and public relations officers and requests may have to be vetted by the head office. Managers are rarely willing to make on the spot decisions.

Although large commercial premises may be unlikely to haggle over a trivial fee they may still show a reluctance to entertain you at all, particularly when you are not the first crew they have encountered. The reason is that you may cost them real money just by your presence. Customers are reluctant to enter a shop or approach a counter where a crew is operating. Cameras, lights and cables can block off whole areas of a shop. Employees who are asked to look busy for the camera are not being busy for the management. Customers looking at the production are not looking at the goods. And inevitably you will start making unreasonable requests.

If an interview or dialogue is involved the recordist will demand that any piped music or public address system be neutralized and telephones taken off the hook. If he doesn't do this he is not doing his job, but the reasons will not be at all clear to people who have no knowledge of the sound problems in film or tape editing. There may even be problems with a buzz or interference from fluorescent lighting, or a hum from the air conditioning system. The electrician is likely to find problems with a mixture of daylight, tungsten and fluorescent lighting and start fiddling around with the standard illumination even before asking to run cables from the main fuse box. The director can only too easily appear to the world as a bullying monster (sometimes he is) by ordering his performers to walk through shot, clear shot, shut up, look animated and repeat actions again and again. For every member of the public who would go to the stake for the chance to appear on television, there are two who would run a mile to avoid being seen.

The quickest way to empty a betting shop or hotel cocktail lounge is to turn up with a camera, largely because of the problem of people who are not where they ought to be and in the wrong company. For this very reason, hotels often charge enormous fees and impose the strictest conditions on television crews. If you want a lounge or bar scene you may have to hire the room and then fill it with paid extras. Social class is no indicator. I once shot a documentary on Dartmoor involving farmhouse cider-making. At the first sight of a camera the rustic workforce melted into the hills. Every one of them had already signed on as unemployed and was drawing the dole.

So you may have to wait until after business hours and re-stage everything. At least this way you will have complete control over sound and light and an optimum flexibility on location. If you are making a drama or dramatized documentary this is the only way to work. But if the operational problems are minimized the financial ones can multiply. Almost certainly you will have to be accompanied throughout by a responsible management figure. Caretakers, security officers and resident electricians may have to be retained beyond normal working hours and, if you are not making a drama but still need extras for realism's sake, you might want to call on other members of staff.

In some circumstances it may be difficult to arrange for such simple amenities as car parks and lavatories to be kept open. Cleaners may have to be delayed or re-scheduled. Automatic security systems may have to be neutralized and the police informed. You may need to make arrangements with a telephone switchboard. In brief a lot of people will very likely be inconvenienced and the minimum price you must pay will be compensation to them and their employers for the overtime and direct expenses involved. And, if you tie people up for lengthy periods, you may find yourself getting involved with personal transport arrangements, taxis, location catering and even paying baby sitters.

Whether drawn up in writing or agreed by telephone you and the owner of the premises are in a contractual relationship and it is your duty as well as your own self interest to fulfil your half of the bargain.

Don't try to lie or fudge the issue when agreeing the hours you need for your production. Every shoot seems to take twice as long as the producer would like, and the bane of experienced cameramen is the young enthusiast director who deliberately ignores the time needed to unpack or pack and move the technical equipment in his shooting schedule. Don't gloss over the real numbers of people involved, or the likelihood of having to move furniture or fixtures. If you confess in advance the scale of the disruption you still have a chance that your pleas of poverty will be heard sympathetically.

If you deceive people the consequences are at the very least that no crew will ever be allowed back or that your story will be abruptly terminated. At worst permission to use your footage may be withheld or you could find yourself victims of a civil action or even in breach of the criminal law.

Private houses

All that has been said about commercial premises can also apply to private houses. Inhabitants of historic locations are these days generally well aware that fees are due for any use of their premises, in fact there are some famously picturesque villages where the visiting crews are seen as a regular source of income.

Ordinary householders may be flattered by the approach of a director. But for even a simple interview the production will routinely rearrange the curtains and the furniture, tamper with the electrics, borrow the telephone, fill the sink with coffee cups, upset the neighbours and give the cat a nervous breakdown.

Be honest. Offer some sort of a fee even if only to cover the cost of the lighting and the chocolate biscuits. If convenient, offer a VHS copy of the item or the programme. If you know that you are doing damage, even if it's just muddy boots on the hall carpet, offer a reasonable cash compensation. It may well be refused but the offer will neutralize all manner of resentments.

A final word of caution. If you are using the same premises more than once, in particular if there is a gap between visits, try to ensure continuity. Even the most squalid householder may suddenly become smitten with a desire to make things look good for the camera. One production was thrown into confusion when the inhabitants of a decayed rat-infested squat managed to get the place freshly wallpapered between successive shooting days.

And, above all else, you *must* be adequately insured, and you *must* be aware of the health and safety obligations of each and every location shoot.

Theatres and concert halls

Theatres and concert halls are appealing locations, but if you don't do your homework they can turn out to be difficult and expensive. Because they are governed by extremely tight fire regulations you cannot assume that you will be able to do exactly what you want with your lights and cables. The many problems inherent in shooting performances or rehearsals involving actors or musicians, of mixing amateurs and professionals or union and non-union personnel, payment and copyright are dealt with below.

If you intend to use such premises in the absence of any kind of performance or public you will still probably have to work with the locally employed technical staff, particularly if you want to use existing lighting, open curtains, or shoot on stage. In this case you need to know if you will incur charges by consulting with the local BECTU union representative.

Location contracts

So far we have assumed the circumstances of fairly straightforward productions and fairly simple location requirements which can be dealt with by *ad hoc* agreements, courtesy, and common sense. But if you are progressing to a complex dramatized production you are well advised to have a more formalized contractual procedure. So put it in writing.

Facility forms

The simplest contract is what was known in the BBC as a facility form. This can be routinely used to pay for premises in most of the sorts of circumstances described above. Where possible the amount is arranged in advance and the director or his PA settle with cash at the end of the shoot. With shoots stretching beyond a day or two, or where very special facilities may be used, or anywhere you are taking over premises to be used for other than their normal daily functions, then you are strongly advised to enter into a more detailed formal contract.

This should at the least take the form of a letter setting out the requirements of the intended shoot, its duration, the specific hours of setting, turning over, and clearing up. The fees should be agreed together with any special limitations or restrictions required by the owner of the location. Both parties should sign copies. If in the course of a drama you or your designer would like to make decorative or structural alterations to a property you should draw up a schedule of the work and allocate time and funds for subsequent restoration to be done either by yourselves or outside contractors. When you have agreed a timetable and costs you must make sure that the owner of the property signs the agreement. Again, it's best to be honest about your needs. If you can see that at the end of the day the room will need redecorating due to production wear and tear or the activities of your designer, ask the owner to get an estimate from a builder or decorator to make it good. You might be able to estimate costs in advance but it is more likely your estimate will have to wait upon the actual damage that's caused. Don't entertain the fond hope that a facility fee also covers damage. The fee is essentially a rent for your use of the premises and compensation for the time taken and inconvenience you have incurred. It in no way implies a compensation for your trail of destruction. Remember many location owners are registered for VAT.

No sensible location proprietor should entertain a visiting crew without proper assurances that he will be covered by an indemnity. A standard wording would be 'X will be responsible for all legal claims for personal injury and damage to property due to its negligence or that of its servants or agents arising directly out of their activities in connection with the production'.

If you are properly insured you will be covered for the smashing of the precious Ming vase in the hallway. Your insurers can impose exclusions and restrictions in the policy and you need to be aware, as with any insurance, of the extent to which you are personally financially liable. Things have to be made crystal clear, particularly in cases where you may be working as an independent on commission to a broadcasting agency or as part of a co-production where some personnel will be covered by a blanket insurance paid for by their employers, while others will not.

If personal injury results from a contravention of health and safety regulations then the director or producer may be liable to criminal prosecution, regardless of any insurance cover. The small print of the policy will probably contain caveats about unnecessary risk.

Fire damage is a frequent fear of property owners and can be a thorny issue for producers and production managers. It may be hard to decide whether a fire which started at the time of shooting was in any way attributable to the presence of the production.

Rather than try to arrange your own cover, which could lead you to all the trouble and cost of a survey, it is better to ask the proprietor to extend his regular insurance for the period of your stay and pay him for any additional premium. Remember to find out how much this will cost.

If you are unlucky and a case of damage or injury does occur you must act exactly as in the case of a traffic accident:

- note down all the circumstances of the incident immediately
- never admit responsibility or offer money
- verify insurance details
- inform your insurance company of the incident as soon as is possible

You will not automatically be covered for all kinds of damage. Drivers of location vehicles have a knack of churning up lawns, shattering paving slabs, or reversing through flower beds. An apology and swift cash compensation might avert wrath. A cast gratuity to a sympathetic gardener or groundsman might ensure the damage is repaired without the owner noticing. But beware. If the damage is extensive a panic offer of a tip to put things right is as good as an admission of guilt in law, and the insurance company may not cover the repair work because of your negligence.

If any of your crew or artists smoke you will have to take extra care. Cigarette burns on a floor or on furniture will be deemed a deliberate act by your insurers. Don't hope to shrug off minor damage as unimportant. A mere scratch or wine stain on the Chippendale table entitles the owner, rightly, to charge you for a complete repolishing of the item. Apart from specific damage, you have a duty to do everything possible to reinstate other people's property after you have finished. Crews from certain programmes/series have acquired reputations rivalled only by that of Atilla the Hun when it comes to the physical and psychological mayhem they leave in their wake.

Remember, if the shoot has been a simple one, try to put everything back exactly as you found it. Clean up kitchens and bathrooms and offer to replace or pay for anything consumed or looted for the production. Empty the ash trays and rearrange the curtains. If you are in a hurry try to leave a team member behind or if necessary send someone back later to help out. On commercial properties, or locations like village halls and schools it is often best, after agreeing your intention with the employer, to offer a reasonable tip to a porter, caretaker or janitor to clear up after you.

Of course there are many locations administered by organizations which have long experience of the ways of visiting production companies. They often have a fixed scale of fees, waiting lists, special insurance conditions, special overtime and security arrangements and safety regulations for the use of lights. Amongst the many are The

National Trust, English Heritage, The National Coal Board, British Waterways, British Rail, The British Library, The Port of London Authority, the Historic Houses Association and most historic universities and major museums. All of these will have established channels for dealing with your application.

There are a number of professional location finding agencies who keep files of all sorts of properties, grand or humble, whose owners welcome television companies. Although they will charge you commission they should have already sorted out the local problems in advance. Most of them advertise in trade periodicals and lists are published in the production services index of the *International Film and Television Year-book*.

Location management is becoming a craft in its own right, and a Guild of Production Managers was established in 1992. As the big broadcast companies continue to shed their support service staff, the role of independent location management agencies will increase. There are already several established agencies whose services range from providing photographic records of available properties to offering a complete on-location service.

If you must go it alone but would like to select from a number of similar locations in a specific area, a good idea is to contact the major local estate agents.

There are frequently selections of domestic and commercial properties either new but unlet, or empty for refurbishment or demolition, which may be available at very little expense. Local housing authorities and regional hospital boards can also be very helpful. Remember, don't make the mistake of turning up without checking that the utilities are working. Empty properties very often have had the electric supply disconnected.

Trespass

These pages have emphasized that you should do your best to keep everyone who might get involved with your production fully informed about your intentions. But there may be times when you find yourselves acting as an interloper either by accident or through taking a reasonable chance. For example, you might be tempted to go for an attractive shot from the top of a hill in the countryside. It may not be a practical proposition to go looking for the landowner. But it always helps to carry a large scale Ordinance Survey map so that you can check footpaths and access points before charging off across the fields.

Contrary to popular opinion there is no general right of privacy in Great Britain. In other words the sign 'Trespassers will be Prosecuted' is what is known by lawyers as a 'wooden falsehood'. Such a sign only expresses the owner's wishes and you would do well to accede to them. But redress for trespass may only be sought by civil action and to prove trespass the plaintiff has to prove direct injury to land, to goods, or to the person. Unless, by leaving gates open, breaking hedges, trampling crops, allowing his dog to run wild, and so on, the trespasser does harm, there can be no grounds for a civil action for damages.

However, trespassers can be requested to depart and be escorted from the land or premises. Reasonable force may be used – reasonable being defined as that commensurate with the amount of resistance put up by the trespasser. This need not take the form of an attack. Remember an assault does not have to end in physical harm. Just threatening someone with a pitchfork constitutes an assault.

Generally the police do not like getting involved with cases involving trespass and are only likely to assist the eviction of trespassers after a court order or where the nature of the invasion of land or privacy is likely to involve more serious offences or provoke an obvious breach of the peace. Of course, if you make a serious nuisance of yourself there are a range of alternative charges the police could bring against you.

None of this applies to property owned by official or semi-official authorities like railways, water companies, local government councils, parks authorities and so on whose rights may be defined by their own by-laws.

Damages for trespass are not likely to be substantial, however the waters become muddied when the issue becomes less one of physical trespass to property than one of trespass to the personal privacy of individuals.

In the past thirty years there have been no fewer than five separate bills before Parliament aimed at making a statutory protection of privacy. All of them have failed to reach the statute book largely because the problems of a definition of privacy appeared to be insuperable. There was also a powerful concurrent argument that any privacy law envisaged would curtail the liberty of the press, although it is widely believed that the excesses of the tabloid press generally provoked the call for new legislation in the first place.

The latest Government Committee on Privacy, the Calcutt Committee, reported in 1990. Although it has made a number of recommendations which should be of more concern to tabloid newspaper hacks than television directors, it did suggest a modification of the laws of trespass. The three main suggestions were that it should be

1. an offence for anyone to enter private property without consent in order to obtain personal information for publication.
2. that it should be illegal to place any surveillance bugging device on private property
3. it should be illegal to take a photograph or make a sound recording of an individual who is on private property without the owner's consent.

At the time of writing no law has been enacted. In fact, if you start planting bugging devices you may be already in contravention of the Wireless and Telegraphy Acts.

Earlier judgements have found that it is not a trespass to shoot activities on private property from public land, nor is it a trespass to shoot private property from an aircraft, however much the object of your attentions might object.

On the other hand there have been cases of gross abuse where journalists have gained access to premises by disguising themselves as meter readers, window cleaners, or the like. In such cases the courts have tended to side with the aggrieved citizens and awarded exemplary punitive damages against the trespassers.

At the beginning of 1993, the issue exploded with the publication of the 'Camillagate' tapes of intercepted telephone conversations involving the Prince of Wales and the suggestion that the Press held much more material such as this up their sleeves. This followed the publication of intimate photographs of the Duchess of York obtained through long lens photography, and the forced resignation of the minister David Mellor over an alleged affair.

The Press and the Government are locked in combat. Any implications for the television programme maker will depend on the outcome.

CHAPTER 2

Out and about

Hells Angels, 1930 Howard Hughes. Still provided by the British Film Institute.

Many of the most seductive shots available to a director can involve using moving cars, boats, planes and helicopters. Yet some of the most notorious disasters in the history of film and television have involved the reckless use of moving vehicles. Although there are obvious safety implications the hazards can be greater than those which immediately meet the eye.

On the road

The normal road traffic regulations are not suspended just because *you* are making a programme. It may be possible to persuade the authorities to suspend some parking regulations or even cone off certain public areas, but driving two abreast down a thoroughfare or staging a motorcycle chase on a public highway is illegal as well as foolhardy.

When filming it is still illegal to drive on the public highway without seatbelts whether or not your famous getaway sequence is ruined by the robbers having to wear them. You may not use fake numberplates on public roads. You may not impersonate police vehicles. Even if you want no more than a few tracking shots through the sunroof of your car, or a sequence of cars driving up or departing it is best to pick a secluded back street or a very quiet time of day, and to inform the local police. Wherever possible you should try to shoot action sequences involving road vehicles on private tracks or roadways. These may not be too hard to locate. There are large numbers of forestry tracks owned both by public bodies and private landlords. There are many small airfields which have perfectly presentable tarmacked perimeter tracks and water companies control many miles of roadway around reservoirs, water works and sewage farms. It is sometimes possible to use complete but unopened stretches of new motorways. Quarry companies, national parks and, of course, the armed forces all control many miles of private highway.

But a private road is much the same as a private house. You will still probably be required to pay a facility fee and you will have to indemnify the owners against all damage. And, of course, the vehicles themselves will have to be fully insured together with the drivers and everyone else involved.

Insurance cannot be over-emphasized. No domestic or normal business insurance is likely to cover the use of a vehicle either as an action property or a camera platform and, of course, it is illegal to drive an uninsured vehicle on a public highway. It is better to use self-drive hire cars rather than cars borrowed from friends or crew members but still the insurance implications have to be confirmed with the hire company.

The large broadcast companies often have blanket insurance arrangements with rental firms for hire cars used by their employees and a commercial sponsor for a corporate video may also be able to provide suitable cover through the company's motor policy. Remember, it is up to you to find out.

Vintage and specialist vehicles can generally be hired, together with all appropriate insurance cover, from a large number of motor museums, specialist collectors, and commercial hire firms. This will not be cheap. Often the vehicles will be supplied with their own drivers and even additional mechanics who will also need paying. Property vehicles will normally be delivered by trailer and often with a drained petrol tank. Safety regulations on film lots and studios usually specify that tanks must be drained to the last pint or so before being admitted to the premises.

A vehicle can be used in a number of ways. When it is just in shot to act as part of the décor, it counts as a dressing property. Don't assume however that it will be immune from damage and the ensuing insurance complications. A carelessly carried tripod can seriously damage the paintwork.

If the vehicle is to be driven in shot it becomes an action property and all the complications suggested above can occur. It may even be wise to consider hiring a stunt driver. An over enthusiastic actor asked just to slam the door of a stationary car can horribly bend the panelling.

The third, and perhaps the commonest use for a vehicle, is to use it as a camera platform. Some cameramen may drive their own vehicles which are insured or even modified for this purpose, but don't count on it. Crew members have a perfect right to refuse to allow any such use of their own vehicles. There is a limited application for handheld shots taken through car windows or from a passenger seat. For really steady shots of people driving you may need to mount the vehicle on the bed of a low loader or tow it with your camera on the vehicle in front. It goes without saying that the highway is not the best place for such shots.

A wide range of fixed camera mounts are available from specialist hire firms at reasonable prices. One of the simplest is the limpet mount. This is a large rubber sucker which can be attached to a car body. Take care when removing this from an old vehicle as you may find yourself liable for a respray bill if the sucker removes a ring of paint.

An almost infinite range of special bracket attachments are available for fixing cameras, and even cameramen, to the bodies of vehicles. Frequently they will be constructed or modified to fit a particular model so do not assume that a suitable one can be immediately picked up off-the-shelf.

Rather than risk affixing any of these yourself you should arrange for a specialist grip to be present. A camera coming adrift at speed because it was not properly attached with the appropriate safety lines could cause injury to personnel and equipment. The only risks you should need to deal with are a certain amount of scratching or bending to the exterior bodywork and minor damage to interior upholstery.

All at sea

The idea of filming on water can be overwhelmingly seductive. It is not within the scope of this book to cover artistic perils but be warned that often the best 'sails in the sunset' shots which seemed ravishing at the time finish up on the cutting room floor. The most exciting sail or power boat race shot under demanding conditions can be a repetitious bore on the small screen.

Above all, do not over-estimate the amount of useful footage you are likely to come home with even after a successful day's shooting. On water everything takes at least twice as long as on land.

Most decent marine or river sequences will require a minimum of two boats, one to be photographed and the other from which to photograph. In many circumstances you may need a third boat to act as a safety tender and to ferry personnel and equipment from ship to shore. If you have no experience of working on water then realize your limitations and plan your shooting in consultation with someone who has the relevant experience. Wind, tides, visibility and local navigational conditions will radically define what you can and cannot achieve. Working with boats is very different from working with road vehicles. You will be very lucky not to encounter mechanical problems. Marine engines, in particular outboards, are notoriously fickle. Salt spray and technical equipment are not good companions. Cameramen who may be experienced sailors often suffer terrible sea sickness when they have to look at a viewfinder for any length of time.

Just accept from the outset that on the anticipated day you may not be able to go to sea at all, or that you might arrive at your station only to be told by your skipper that you have to turn round and run for home. Putting to sea against the advice of experts who may have to rescue you is not to be advised.

Boat hire

There are three ways in which you can hire boats. Hire and sail the vessel yourself, charter a craft with its skipper and crew, or charter a craft just to appear in vision without placing your production crew on board.

You shouldn't think of hiring a vessel unless you and the crew are proficient. Even if you are taking out a canal narrowboat on five feet of water you should have made a thorough recce and familiarized yourself with both the operation of the craft and the rules for inland navigation. The day of the shoot is no time to start working out how to raise bridges or operate a lock windlass. For a good sequence you will certainly have to repeat actions as in any other kind of single camera shooting. Do you really want to take a boat through a lock twice?

Work out where you are going to, how you are going to get there, how to turn round, and how long the whole trip will take you. On tidal waters one of the production crew must be qualified, and the skipper should preferably have a Yachtmaster's Certificate. Remember, shooting from boats will often require more complex manoeuvres than those required of the average weekend sailor.

If you can charter a vessel without a skipper then for insurance purposes the boat becomes a 'property'. It is your responsibility to return it in the condition which it was delivered to you, in addition to paying the hire charge and any agreed arrangements about fuel costs, harbour dues, or berthing expenses. It is up to you to arrange full insurance including third party for the vessel, the production team, and any boat crew.

You can charter a craft together with its own skipper and crew. In this case the production crew travel as passengers in the eyes of the law. The boat itself is now regarded as a location facility in the same way as a hired premises on land. This means that you must agree an indemnity to the boat owner for any damage you might cause and in addition you should check the owner's marine insurance. Watch for the following:

- Is the owner fully insured for damage to the hull, machinery and equipment? If the policy doesn't cover this he must agree that he operates at his own risk.

- Does his liability extend to passengers on his boat, i.e. you and your team?

- Does he carry third party liability?

The risks may seem reduced with small boats on inland waters but beware. Often these owners have not taken adequate insurance cover and your activities might therefore put property and persons at risk.

If you wish to charter a craft to appear in shot without placing your production crew on board, you must check that the owner and those with him are fully insured and accept the terms of an appearance fee. Unless you are recording an event like a real race you will probably want to direct the actions of the boats concerned. Normally the skipper will rely upon his own judgement about the reasonableness of your requests, but if you make risky demands which end in grief in the eyes of the insurance company you will be liable. Under current health and safety rules both you and the skipper will be liable to criminal prosecution.

This all sounds formidable but you are only likely to run into real trouble when you try to cut corners by informally contracting privately owned vessels. In many harbours and tidal waters there are recognized boatmens' associations whose members are fully cognisant of safety and insurance considerations, who carry the requisite navigational aids, and are licensed for passengers.

On some waters, such as the tidal Thames, you may only shoot from a hired craft if it is skippered by a licensed waterman.

Remember that fuel is costly and harbour and berthing fees are easily run up. Even tiny harbours may levy a harbour due every time your craft enters harbour, however small the craft and however brief the turn-around time. Marinas are costly if not rapacious, and you will have to pay for berthing even for a matter of hours.

If you leave territorial waters you must declare yourselves to H.M. Customs and Excise on your return.

Safety

Charter vessels should be automatically equipped with regulation life jackets, life rafts and fire safety aids. When you are shooting documentary material about craft which are not normally passenger carrying, such as small inshore fishing or pleasure craft, you will need to take special care.

All members of your team should either wear life jackets or have easy access to them and know how to use them. This applies to inland reservoirs no less than the high seas. In the case of racing boats, or wherever the cameraman is unable to hold on and is unprotected by a rail, safety harnesses may be needed.

Find out if any of your team are non-swimmers and insist that they wear life preservers at all times. Take special care with any artists wearing costume likely to encumber them should they fall in.

Every year people drown in less than six feet of water. Make sure that you always have access to old fashioned lifebuoys and lines during your shoot even if you are just on a quayside or canal bank. If you are shooting drama on the water you may need to hire a safety diver or have one of your crew always dressed and ready to go in. At least one of you ought to know about basic life saving methods, resuscitation and first aid.

Check the availability of fire extinguishers and if you have any doubts bring your own, particularly if any special effects are involved.

Check communications systems before you set out. You will need your own walkie talkies as well as access to ship-to-shore radio. Check frequencies before beginning. Increasingly craft are obliged to carry radio communications, for example large river or canal craft venturing into the tidal stretches of the Thames.

The first rule is whenever working in unfamiliar waters seek out local advice. Coastguards, harbourmasters, lifeboat coxswains, meteorological stations and air sea rescue services will all advise you. Buy yourself a set of tidetables and an admiralty chart and learn how to recognize basic navigation marks.

Finally, remember that working at sea, or even on the shore, requires even more care than filming in a city street.

Never simulate any kind of an incident without alerting all the relevant authorities including the local harbour authorities, police and rescue services. Never fire rockets or set off maroons. Never hoist incorrect flags, sound fake alarms or give misleading signals. Do not use flame or smoke effects at sea and never simulate capsizings, drownings or cliff accidents without making sure that no member of the public will spot you and raise the alarm. Remember a lot of people use binoculars. Tomfoolery leading to a needless launch of a lifeboat or the arrival of a rescue helicopter will not be appreciated by the rescue services.

Up and away

The idea of glamorous aerial shots has an even more mesmeric appeal than sailing sequences to some directors.

Aircraft hire

There are a number of commercial companies who specialize in aerial photographic work from light aircraft, helicopters, balloons and dirigibles. They all have fully qualified pilots who are experienced in the manoeuvres needed to obtain good camera shots and are able to advise on the meteorological and light conditions likely to give you the best results. Several can provide highly sophisticated camera mountings with gyroscopically stabilized and computer controlled equipment. They may also provide their own skilled camera operators. The costs are high. The most ravishing aerial sequences are frankly likely to be only within the pockets of feature film or commercial advertising producers.

There may be occasions, though, when aerial photography is required by a production with only a modest budget.

There are four categories of pilot licences – the Private Pilots Licence (PPL), the Commercial Pilots Licence (CPL), the Senior Commercial Pilots Licence (SCPL) and the Aircraft Transport Pilots Licence (ATPL). Only the last three of these may fly for reward. In other words you may not charter an ordinary private flyer to take you up.

If you hire an aircraft you must therefore find someone with a commercial licence. Your best bet is to start by asking a commercially licensed flying instructor or the air traffic controllers at a small airfield who will be a mine of information about who is qualified or likely to agree to what. Unless you are very lucky and come up with a friendly ATPL airline pilot who is also a hobby flier you will probably find that commercially qualified fliers will want the full commercial rate for their services. This is usually based on an hourly rate for flying lessons and may be more if you are asking anything out of the ordinary. If you are planning a lengthy shoot you should shop around and negotiate.

Although the holder of an ordinary Private Pilots License may not accept payment he can offer you a ride as a passenger and you may come to an understanding about sharing the fuel bill. Before jumping at such an offer think about exactly what you need. Few light aircraft accommodate more than a couple of passengers, and often there is only room for one plus a camera. If two of the team can reasonably go up, the director has to decide which two. It is possible, if the sequence involves shooting inside the cockpit as well as through the window, that the director is better replaced by a fully briefed recordist. Any member of the crew has the absolute right to refuse to go if he has the least qualm about the pilot or the craft.

Check the competence of the pilot. The BBC suggests that directors ask the pilot to produce his log book. As a minimum during the previous thirteen months, he should have flown at least three hundred hours with a minimum of twenty-five hours as pilot-in-command.

If you still have reservations go to a senior flying instructor, air traffic controller or president of the local flying club. Flyers are aware that there are old pilots and there are bold pilots but there are no old, bold pilots. They can be blunt about each others shortcomings in the air.

As with boats you may charter a plane for a performance without any of your team being passengers. In this case you should charter a suitable model and ensure that the pilot holds a commercial licence and is fully insured for your purposes. Most pilots will be insured but they will not have anticipated television productions and their third party liability, particularly third party liability on the ground, may not be adequate cover in the opinion of your own employers or insurance company. Take advice. Mistakes involving aircraft tend to be lethal.

With or without a cameraman on board simple take-off, landing, and straight flying sequences should pose no problems so long as the pilot keeps air traffic control fully informed of his activities. But for anything out of the ordinary you must comply with special civil aviation regulations and this means obtaining written permission from the Civil Aviation Authority. *It is the responsibility of the television production company, not the responsibility of the pilot, to ensure that CAA clearance has been granted.*

Directors usually want low altitude flying, eccentric navigation and the overflight of built-up areas. However, the safe altitude at which aircraft are permitted to be flown, the areas open to private traffic and the routes to be flown, are very strictly controlled.

Remember:

- No fixed wing plane is permitted to fly over built up areas lower than fifteen hundred feet above the tallest structure or so low as not to be able to make a safe touch down in the open in the event of engine failure.

- helicopters are forbidden from flying at under 1,500 feet over any human settlement without the specific written permission of the CAA and helicopter flight paths, particularly over London, are subject to stringent controls.

- In no circumstances may an aircraft fly closer than 500 feet to any person, vehicle or building.

- When flying over a city you may be obliged to use a twin-engined aircraft.

Don't let your imagination run away with you. Unless they are realistically planned, flying sequences can be disappointing when viewed in the edit suite and it's worse knowing that it's cost a lot of money.

On the ground

Even working with aeroplanes on the ground can be uncommonly hazardous. The pilot of a taxiing plane often cannot see the ground immediately in front of him nor can he hear anything except through his earphones, so be very careful when trying to get shots of planes manoeuvring on the tarmac.

Remember:

- Never go near the propeller of a stationary plane particularly if there is any chance of the engine being warm. A mere shove could start it up.

- Never get involved in handling planes or gliders on the ground, leave it to people who know what they are doing.

- Make sure that you clear with the airport management and air traffic control any plans you have for shooting from the ends of runways, turning areas, or perimeter roadways. In some cases there may be safety or government security reasons why you will be refused access to areas.

Remember that airfields are a complex of different commercial enterprises. The airfield management may give you permission to film but you will have to negotiate separately with the various individual flying schools, clubs, charter firms, shipping agents, maintenance workshops and so on.

Finally, remember never to allow cigarettes or matches anywhere near aviation fuel.

In the air

Safety considerations are paramount.

The director should always prepare a list of shots, perhaps with the help of a storyboard, and agree these with the pilot. In the air the flyer is going to have enough to worry about without having in-flight discussions about shot sizes. Work out in advance a simple set of instructions or hand signals for communication between the cameraman and the pilot. In fixed wing planes the visibility of both pilot and cameraman is restricted by the wings so it is particularly important to remember this when you are hoping to shoot from plane to plane in the air. Have everything perfectly worked out and agreed before you take off or the pilot may quite rightly refuse to perform the manoeuvres needed to get the camera angles you envisage. Check that you are shooting when the angle of the sun suits your purpose. You don't want the low sun right into the lens, on the other hand summer landscapes often show their relief to best advantage either early or late when the shadows pick out the details.

Decide how the crew and equipment are to be deployed inside the plane. Light aircraft have to be balanced properly and are not good places for sudden changes of seating arrangements. You may find that you want to shoot with the door removed, in which case the cameraman has to be satisfied with the safety harnesses and if the camera is to poke into the slipstream proper safety lines will be needed. If at all possible try to go for a dummy run before finalizing your shots. If two planes are involved make absolutely sure that both pilots are experienced in formation flying. The golden rule is that the plane carrying the cameraman should maintain a level pre-arranged flight path and that all manoeuvering should be left to the planes being shot. In no circumstances should they underfly the camera plane. And check that the two craft have compatible flying speeds. A plane trying to fly below its designed speed risks stalling.

If flying over water make sure that everyone is aware of the ditching drill and see that enough life jackets are carried. If working with or near jet aircraft issue your crew with ear defenders. Both helicopters and light aircraft are prone to vibration and CAA altitude regulations will probably oblige you to shoot on the end of a zoom lens thus further emphasizing camera shake. For a news or current affairs programme this may not matter, but for a drama or a poetic evocation of the countryside the effect can be ruinous and you need to ask yourself whether you need, or can afford, specially gyroscopically stabilized equipment.

When hiring equipment remember that insurance firms may count aerial photography as an unacceptably hazardous activity and you should check your cover and your agreement with the rental company before setting out.

At the time of writing the cost of hiring a helicopter is around £400–

£1000 per hour depending on size. When hiring a helicopter you may be advised to take the services of a flight engineer as well as a pilot. This will be money well spent as he will be able to perform minor technical adjustments with seats or doors and will be responsible for the fixing and removal of any camera mounts.

Even when you have every CAA clearance and agreement from your pilot be wary about deciding to put down your helicopter in open country without planning and the agreement of the landlord. A flock of panicked ewes in lamb for instance can result in expensive consequences.

CHAPTER 3

Going foreign

Shooting on an overseas location has tremendous appeal. The opportunities for travel, particularly at someone else's expense, is one of the great attractions of a career in television, however many practitioners fairly soon decide that the pursuit of the exotic is something they can happily do without. There is a world of difference between setting off alone with a stills camera in your holdall, and carting crates of equipment around, whose movements you are obliged to document in detail, taking a crew who succumb to every local infection, and working to a budget which becomes the target for every extortionate hotelier, taxi driver, guide and customs officer for miles around. Either you'll have the temperament for it or you won't.

Getting there

Overseas travel usually involves long delays and bureaucratic hitches. Always give yourself plenty of travel time and an adequate budget.

Baggage

Never forget that professional film and video equipment is heavy and that excess baggage charges on airlines can be crippling. Baggage may be calculated by an airline either by weight or by volume. At a rough guess you should reckon on about one and a half times the return first class fare to your destination for a set of camera, recording and lighting equipment plus the tape or film stock needed for a basic three man documentary team.

You may prefer to travel by road or rail where possible but these modes of transport also have their own disadvantages and the savings you could make on excess baggage payments may be negated by the extra travel time involved.

Sometimes it is possible to negotiate special cheap 'all-in' deals with airlines so it is always worth approaching the appropriate carriers direct and comparing prices. If you do a deal over excess baggage with even the largest of airlines check that the special rate applies to both the outward journey and return journey. Don't expect the two charges to automatically tally. Remember that the airlines most likely to offer bargains are those with the biggest difficulty in filling their aeroplanes. There may be good reasons for their lack of popularity.

Seasoned travellers will spend happy hours swapping tales of the East European airline prone to lengthy stopovers in Siberia where passengers were parted from all their available hard currency, the African airline forbidden from touching down in one of its own airports for nonpayment of fuel bills, or the Arab line which specializes in transporting air sick pilgrims on which neither food nor drink is available.

On long haul flights it is well worth the effort to get seats up-graded to the equivalent of Club or Business class. If you are employing a well-travelled crew they will have had enough of the glamour of flight, and ten or twelve hours crammed into seats for dwarves with abysmal food will just result in bad backs and bad tempers. It can even be cheaper to fly first class to take advantage of the much greater baggage allowances.

Hiring local crews and equipment

One solution might seem to be the hire of local crews and equipment. Alas, this is only a solution if you can be absolutely sure of the calibre of your technicians and the reliability and compatibility of their equipment – a particularly important point when shooting on videotape. If you do employ a foreign crew you need to have a contract drawn up in advance. This is probably only feasible if you deal direct via a known company used to dealing with foreign crews, or a local broadcasting station with reciprocal agreements.

Local freelance crews may charge for every meal taken, every kilometre travelled, and every hour of overtime locally calculated. You can be charged highly for every microphone battery or roll of camera tape used. Many a producer has been all but bankrupted through underestimating local freelance charges.

If you use local facilities does it matter to you if their system is on PAL, NTSC, or one of the SECAM standards? If you are taking your own lights does your destination work to a 240 or 110 volt system? Do the locals use a compatible tape stock or is appropriate film stock locally provided?

Taking your own equipment

For the import and re-export of technical equipment many countries demand a carnet which is a sort of passport for goods. Most countries, including our own, charge hefty duties on technical equipment being imported, and in some countries the tax is even greater than the original purchase price in the UK. Moreover if you leave home without declaring your precious Japanese equipment to the British customs, and having evidence of purchase and taxes paid, you are liable to be pounced on for import duty and VAT on your return.

The carnet is intended to avoid such problems. It details all the equipment your crew will be carrying, showing serial numbers, technical description, and value. It contains a number of tear-out sheets and as you leave or enter any country the local customs will check the technical gear against the list provided. This means that you dare not pass through an airport or cross a frontier without having the carnet formalities completed. Often you will be hanging around for hours waiting for the responsible authorities to check all is in order by unpacking your boxes, having you painstakingly explain what everything is and then repacking. Even then your carnet will only cover the equipment, and the customs may yet prove sticky over film and tape stock, batteries, and any costumes or properties you are carrying.

Carnets are issued by large local Chambers of Commerce and can be applied for direct or via your shipping agent. It may take several days to prepare and you cannot subsequently alter or substitute items of equipment. There is a not inconsiderable fee for preparing a carnet and you will also have to put down a security to the estimated value of your equipment which will be forfeit if the items are not returned to the United Kingdom. The security should be in the form of a guaranteed bank deposit or insurance agreement. The carnet will only remain valid for one year but the bills for duties and fines levied by customs authorities may take as long as a couple of years to surface.

Some countries insist on carnets, some regard them as discretionary but can make life difficult for those who do not carry them, and some may accept a simpler procedure. Seeking the advice of a good shipping agent, preferably one with experience of television crews, is essential.

Countries which do not insist on carnets will often accept a simple typewritten list of all the equipment complete with values, serial numbers and countries of origin. Provide the British Customs with two copies before departure. They will stamp one copy which will be returned to you and will keep the second copy on file against your return. Life then gets difficult when your outward flight is from Heathrow and your return is diverted to Manchester. You should keep a large sheaf of similar copies and repeat the procedure on each arrival. Some countries refuse to accept photocopies and others may ask for copies in translation. You may have to be prepared for a demand for a bond or bank guarantee against the re-export of the equipment. If possible you should get agreement from your sponsors or the local tourist office or a government organization to stand surety for you during your shooting. The problems which ensue when your assistant drops the tripod in the Amazon or your recorder is stolen can be imagined. At such times the services of your local 'fixer' will be truly appreciated.

You might be tempted to despatch your equipment by air freight. There is not likely to be much of a saving compared with sharing out personal baggage allowances and paying the excess if you are a small unit. However, you will still need carnets, packing lists and a local forwarding agent to clear everything through customs. Without your personal attention delays of several days are normal and items may go missing. Using a freight carrier is probably only a sensible option for drama productions burdened by large amounts of non-technical material. Even then you may find that some cameramen will not be separated from their cameras and will insist on taking them as hand baggage. Certain kinds of primitive X-ray machines and other security equipment can damage electronic equipment, film and tape stock.

There is one encouraging development. From the beginning of 1993 there will no longer be border checks within the countries of the EEC. However, you would still be advised to keep to hand a typewritten list of your equipment even after 1992. Local difficulties are still likely to arise after all internal barriers have, in theory, been swept away. VAT has still to be harmonized.

Remember that certain items of equipment are restricted in certain countries. Computer hardware and software may not, at the time of writing, be taken to the Peoples' Republic of China. For a long period there were restrictions on the transport of any equipment containing microchips to Eastern block European countries. There are sweeping embargoes on what may be taken legally to designated hostile countries in the Middle East. If you are in doubt about what you may take to your chosen destination contact the Board of Trade to see what export licences are needed.

Airlines impose their own restrictions. Those belonging to the International Air Traffic Association (IATA) which includes most of the big international carriers, have a common set of rules. Items which can cause problems include weapons, whether fake or real, spirit-based solvents and cosmetics, aerosols, pyrotechnics, alcohol, medicines, animals or animal products. Because of the risk of terrorism there are also problems with the transport of electrical and electronic equipment in luggage stowed in the hold and, with the generation of computer flown aircraft, there are restrictions on electrical equipment in hand luggage which might interfere with the navigational equipment. Breaches of both Board of Trade and IATA regulations will result in missing the flight, and possible fines or imprisonment if you are caught in Great Britain. The consequences if you get caught overseas may be worse.

Employing a 'fixer'

In non English speaking countries and countries outside Europe you are well advised to find and employ a local 'fixer' i.e. someone who knows about television crews, speaks the local languages, can win over the support of the native bureaucracy and knows how to bargain for transport and obtain official permits.

Good fixers are worth their weight in gold, even when it feels as if this is how they have to be paid! Sometimes fixers will be government employees, in which case extra payment may be agreed to turn them from official minders into allies. Sometimes they may be freelance journalistic stringers or even taxi drivers. Names get passed from production team to production team. Before embarking on a costly foreign adventure always try to locate someone who has recently been to your destination and pick his brains.

One warning for those going it alone for the first time. There are countries where it is normal for officials to supplement their salaries by exacting private contributions, and this can extend from traffic policemen and receptionists to museum directors and ministry officials. The methods can range from extortion at gunpoint to a pointed request for the purchase of lottery tickets. The most usual tactic is to refuse permission for you to shoot anywhere without protracted delays and unexplained bureaucratic procedures. How you cope with this depends on your moral integrity, the urgency of your deadline, and the depth of your pocket.

Local transport

Local transport needs careful costing. Self-drive cars are comparatively cheap and simply arranged in the UK but this is not always the case elsewhere. Local staff who provide their own cars may have their own ideas about the costs of mileage, fuel and insurance and you need some idea of the implications in advance. The mechanical condition of vehicles provided locally may be so awful that an expensive agreement with one of the international car hire companies may be your only safe course of action. In many countries you will find it essential to hire local drivers with each vehicle and in the Republic of China for instance, visitors are not allowed to drive themselves. Often government agencies will provide drivers. Check they have enough insurance cover.

Although local driving skills and etiquette may not be for the fainthearted, the advantages of using local drivers can be substantial as they are held responsible if there is an accident. Even in some European countries the driver of a vehicle involved in a serious accident may be thrown into jail pending an enquiry or court proceedings. In some other countries an accident involving a death or serious injury may be swiftly followed by the public lynching of the offending driver.

If you do intend to drive yourselves check that everyone involved holds an acceptable driving licence. The recent EEC style British driving licence is accepted by most countries but the older type may not be, although it is still valid in the UK. Some countries insist on an international driving permit which includes a photograph. You can purchase these from any branch of the AA or the RAC. Plans have been announced for the next generation of British driving licences to carry photographs and meet all international requirements. Although your driving licence may be valid take care to check that your insurance cover is sufficient for your needs.

In the USA third party cover may be as low as $25,000. As a consequence many hire companies offer an additional cover of $1 million. Despite the additional expense it is well worth taking up.

It is also worth checking any other local restrictions. In some countries, and certain states of the USA, insurance cover becomes invalid if a driver involved in any accident has any trace of alcohol in his bloodstream. Women may not drive in Saudi Arabia.

Visas

Many countries will demand visas for entry. The lack of visa requirements usually means that there is a bilateral agreement between the nations concerned to scrap them. In some cases a visa is a mere formality and short stay visas will be issued automatically on arrival at your destination. In many other cases you will have to make individual approaches to the nearest appropriate consulate to complete papers and pay fees, which are sometimes expensive. There is often a delay of days or weeks and, in some cases, you will be asked to make a personal appearance at the consulate. Some consulates accept payment by cash only. Many are very sensitive about journalists and television crews and your application may be delayed for weeks or rejected outright depending on the diplomatic mood of the moment.

Main travel agents may be able to arrange the collection of visas and carry application forms for the commonest ones and in London there are commercial organizations who will, for a fee, undertake the visiting of embassies on your behalf. But make sure that they are aware that you are not travelling as normal tourists or businessmen.

You must check the validity of the passports of every member of your team. Remember there are different types of British passports depending on the birthplace and origins of the bearer. A Republic of Ireland passport for example, seems a wonderful opener of doors, and is available to those of immediate Irish antecedents. At the time of writing France demands visas from citizens of certain non EEC countries resident in the UK so if any of your team were born in New Zealand, for example, they need to make prior application. Airlines are particularly vulnerable to the consequences of diplomatic upsets since they are held responsible for transporting illegally documented passengers and may have to repatriate them. Hence they may refuse to carry you unless your visas are in order.

Even when you get a visa you may not be out of the woods. It may only entitle you to enter the country and stay for a very limited time. You may only be able to start an application for an extension and permission to start work after you have landed. In some countries there is official supervision, censorship and legal restrictions on your work. In others there may be trades union agreements involving you in an obligation to hire or train local broadcasting staff, or possibly hire a local 'shadow' crew. The use of actors may be restricted by the agreements between different national Actors' Equity unions. You may be required to submit a written screenplay, or list of contributors, or agree an itinerary before getting permission to film.

A recent technological development has been the production of highly sophisticated but extremely small videotape formats capable of producing results of nearly broadcast quality. To the uninformed eye there is no obvious distinction between some of these and the average tourist's home camcorder. This gives rise to the temptation to short circuit all the potential problems, and travel in the guise of holiday makers. This has sometimes been the only way where dissidents in police states have been contacted and recorded. Apart from the risks involved in shooting politically sensitive subjects in areas normally out of bounds, there can be artistic as well as logistical problems. You may not need lights, a tripod, or professional quality camera and microphones, but if you use home movie methods you are likely to achieve only home movie standards.

Taking children to work overseas

Children, i.e. persons under the age of eighteen, may be taken abroad to work as performers only upon the issue of a special licence. Notice must be given to the Chief Constable for the district in which the minor lives and there should be consultation with the local licensing authority, usually the Local Education Authority. Licences in London are issued by the Chief Magistrate at Bow Street.

The regulations for children going to work in the role of fashion models or to make sound recordings are different but they are also subject to a range of by-laws concerning the employment of children. As with anything to do with children the legal position is fiendishly complicated. If you are determined to take a minor overseas your best guide is the HMSO publication *The Law on Performances by Children*. Don't forget that the country you are visiting will have its own laws about the employment of minors and these might be even more restrictive than the British ones. For example in Austria children are prohibited from working in television commercials, and their place is taken by professional dwarf actors.

Health

Travelling abroad involves health risks, particularly if your production takes you to hot places and away from the sanitized environs of the tourist hotel.

The main health risks come from insect carried diseases like malaria and yellow fever, and water-borne ones like typhoid and cholera. Polio and hepatitis are serious additional risks. It also has to be remembered that a couple of generations have grown up in Britain with little exposure, and therefore no resistance, to a whole range of once common infections. For example, few Westerners bother to be vaccinated against tuberculosis although it remains rampant in parts of the tropics and indeed some cities in the USA, as do once universal childhood infections like measles. For some of these inoculations may be appropriate. For others like the 'Gippy Tummy', 'Bombay Belly', or the 'Aztec Two Step' there is no precaution which will save the first-time traveller, and as a producer you will have to accept and plan for possible delays caused by minor ailments on location.

Inoculation certificates are obligatory for those travelling to or from many countries, particularly those in Africa and South America. For certain inoculations the certificate is not valid until a fixed period from the first of a course of injections has elapsed, so don't leave medical precautions until the eve of departure. Other inoculations last only a short time and it is wise to keep your booster jabs up to date if you hope to travel frequently. Some countries like Saudi Arabia may insist on a certificate showing that the bearer is not HIV positive. Don't forget that regulations concerning people flying from the United Kingdom to another country do not necessarily cover travel from that country to a third one. In other words make sure that everyone has a complete valid set of health certificates to avoid the risk of being refused entry to a country or getting a seat on an airline.

Individual countries change their requirements from time to time. Travel agents will know about the main holiday destinations but there has been a tendency in the past for them to play down or ignore health hazards so as not to put off their more nervous customers. If you have a complex itinerary check health regulations with the International Relations branch of the Department of Health and Social Security.

The disease giving most concern at the moment is malaria. Not only is malaria returning to places such as the Mediterranean region where it had been thought to be defeated, but it has shown the ability to mutate and build up strains resistant to existing prophylactics. There are places where not one, but two or three courses of pills must be taken. Some of these new strains can cause cerebral malaria and are killers. Your local GP may not be up to date as the advice can change from month to month. The World Health Organization is constantly up-dating health advice and current information is fed into the central computer of the London School of Hygiene and Tropical Medicine. The Medical Advisory Service for Travellers Abroad (MASTA) updates its database daily, and in conjunction with British Airways has set up a network of clinics across the country. Their great advantage, apart from giving the latest advice, is that all the requisite injections are available under one roof, and preventative and care items are available which you are not able to buy at a high street chemist. These include mosquito nets for sleeping quarters and to be worn with hats, insect repellent impregnated wrist and ankle bands, water purification equipment, and dental emergency packs.

Increasingly vital is a pack of hypodermics and sterile needles for both injections and simple stitches. The risk of accidentally getting AIDS or hepatitis B from unsterilized medical equipment cannot be ignored. Currently there are twenty-seven such clinics and more are planned. Many are open six days a week and in the evenings. You are advised to make an appointment.

CHAPTER 4

Cast, crew and other animals

Tarzan finds a Son, 1939. © 1939 (MGM). Still provided by the British Film Institute.

So far we have been concerned mainly with the directors and their immediate staff, the technical crews, and the members of the public. But even a simple production may need the services of actors, presenters or other amateur or professional performers. Working with performing artists can lead to many other pitfalls.

Casting

Many presenters or commentators, whether appearing in vision or as a voice-over, are not subject to any union negotiated scale of fees or conditions of employment, so you will have to negotiate such performers yourself. However there are also local agreements between broadcast companies and members of the National Union of Journalists and British Actors' Equity setting minimum rates.

Professional actors and actresses will normally be members of Equity and appearance upon the professional stage or broadcast television is usually conditional upon the performers holding Equity membership. This is usually obtained by undergoing training at a recognized stage school followed by a number of probationary performances. There are however a number of other ways of getting membership, including having started a career as a public performer – pop singers and variety or circus entertainers fall into this category. So whether your ambitions are Shakespearean, or involve jugglers and strippers, you need to check union membership. Normally, Equity members will refuse to work alongside non-Equity performers, so if you foresee any possibility of bringing together professional and non-professional performers in the same production, sort the situation out with the union first.

Because of reciprocal union agreements and restrictions you should be very careful when employing foreign performers, in particular American ones. The bible of all casting directors is the annually revised directory of all British actors and actresses *Spotlight*. It includes the photographs of all performers, brief career details and addresses for their theatrical agents. Most performers, though not all, may be contracted through their agents. There are Equity minimum rates for rehearsals and for performances but the lowest rates are very low indeed. On the other hand only the few actors and actresses at the top of the ladder can rely on regular and lucrative work and many may take the attitude that it is better to take a short, poorly paid job rather than not work at all.

All approaches should be made via the agent but there may be times when an agent is keen to build up the prestige and market value of the client and will turn down your approach as being unsuitable. If you make a personal friendly approach to the artist and suspect that he or she may be particularly interested in your script you might persuade your performer to accept less than the usual anticipated fee. But be careful with any informal approaches. A verbal contract by telephone is still a contract even if, as Sam Goldwyn is reputed to have said, 'a verbal contract ain't worth the paper it's written on.'

Start your enquiries with an availability check and make it clear to the agent that availability is all that you are currently checking. If your approach is along the lines of 'Hello, Sir Ralph, would you be free to play King Lear between the 10th and the 21st?' you have in effect contracted him. If subsequently he turns down other offers whilst you change the dates or contract Sir Donald instead, you will be in breach of contract.

There is probably nowhere in the world which has such a huge number of really excellent actors, little recognized outside the profession, with both stage and camera experience as the UK. One word of caution. There has been an enormous inflation of fees in two specific areas which affects both Equity and non-Equity performers. The first of these is the television commercial, which often involves enormous fees and residuals, but where clients apparently expect to spend astronomic sums. The second is, surprisingly, the corporate video. Many businessmen are convinced that the presence in one of their videos of a recognizable newsreader, reporter or actor gives immediate prestige to their product, or that a well-known voice in commentary automatically enhances its integrity. Many broadcast television performers can double or treble their salaries through bumping up the fees of rarely seen corporate commissions. If you have serious budgetary restraints it can be as well to shop around the many thoroughly professional performers who have not attained the status of public celebrity but who will probably turn in a more competent and enthusiastic job for you.

On the other hand there are times when for various reasons you might wish to use amateurs. There are for example a number of historic battle re-enactment societies which are capable of laying on hundreds or even thousands of fully equipped and costumed performers complete with artillery. These have worked out scales of fees depending on the scale of the production required. There are many lesser groups of enthusiasts, of varying degrees of eccentricity, who specialize in dressing up as engine drivers, crusaders, mediaeval outlaws and the characters in Rembrandt's painting of *The Night Watch*. You can negotiate collectively or with the individuals concerned. Some may be delighted to work for nothing. Just remember that you cannot count on using them in a dramatic context alongside professional actors. Also make sure that the insurance implications are quite clear. Enthusiastic amateurs are more likely than professionals to turn up in inflammable costumes or with unsafe pyrotechnics and carry unblunted swords.

There will be cases where you will want to employ proper extras in a production, either for full blown dramas or for historical documentary purposes. The main broadcast organizations have agreements to employ Equity members to act as extras, but the extras employed by feature film companies and most independent television productions are represented by the Film Artistes Association (FAA). The FAA will provide lists of members available as extras in a particular region. Productions try as far as possible to cut costs by employing local extras and many a crowd scene location has been chosen with an eye to the number of FAA and Equity members known to be available in the district.

Avoid mixing union and non-union employees, and don't pay differential rates on the same production even if the local dramatic society offers to swell your crowd scenes for next to nothing. You are usually expected to employ only union members if you are shooting within forty miles of London. Outside this limit you will be allowed to employ members of the public so long as you have given priority to the available union members in the first instance, and have informed the relevant union.

Extras

Extras come in three categories. Supporting artistes are basically faces in the crowd. They should not be expected to utter any dialogue beyond improvised background 'rhubarb' crowd noises. They will usually be expected to wear appropriate contemporary dress as part of their services and many of them will have their own wardrobe for specialist scenes, e.g. their own evening dress or service uniforms. If they are asked to come specially attired you will have to pay extra accordingly although this will work out cheaper than fitting and hiring dress from a costumiers. A perennial problem is getting appropriate hairstyles. For example, anything portraying servicemen in the Second World War would need male extras to wear the short-back-and-sides haircut of the period, a military uniform cap cannot disguise another style. If you want your extras to get appropriate haircuts you have to make it clear to them or their agents what is required in advance. If they turn up on location and can claim that no haircut clause was mentioned in their contracts they may refuse to cooperate and you will have to take them looking as they are, or pay them regardless and send them home. If they have accepted a haircut clause they are in breach of contract if they refuse to be shorn, however there are union agreements which allow for extra payments where extras are asked to submit to haircuts which are regarded as too short or extreme in style for the fashions of the day. The other categories of extras are walk-ons (one) and walk-ons (two). Both may expect slightly higher fees than simple supporting artistes. A walk-on (one) may still only utter 'rhubarb-rhubarb' dialogue but is expected to portray a specific role, for example a recognizable check-out cashier, village shopkeeper, police constable or whatever. In brief they perform an individual role directed as part of a scene and normally will require full costume and make-up. Because they can be expected to take individual direction, it is best to employ all your extras on these terms and accept the slight extra expense. A walk-on (two) may be expected both to be directed and to utter lines of dialogue so long as these are not in the script or specifically vital to the dramatic action. In other words audible conversation in a pub or improvised chat over the telephone in an office set up will be OK so long as the actors are not asked to react to specific dialogue. The difference in pay between full Equity members on the minimum rate, and the categories of extras, is not very great, so you are probably advised to employ actors and actresses where few members are involved. Then if you want to write in script lines or extra dramatic business you may do so. There are local agreements between Equity and the broadcasting companies covering overtime, rehearsal fees and repeat payments. You may find that supporting artistes may be contracted for a flat fee, whilst your walk-ons (one) or (two) might qualify for residual payments. Both you and your artistes need to be clear about the deal involved before starting production.

If you want your extras to perform special skills – and driving a car in shot or sitting on a horse count as skills – you have to specify them in advance and will have to make an additional standard payment. If these skills involve any risk you will be expected to employ registered stunt artists. It's one thing to ask your extra to sit on his horse, another to ask him to participate in a cavalry charge or take the beast over the sticks. Special skills allowances apply to female performers who are asked to appear topless and to artists of either sex asked to appear nude.

If your extras are required to perform what they claim as arduous work or appear in conditions of unusual discomfort, you may have to negotiate additional payments. If you want to recreate a scene from trench warfare or a Siberian forced labour camp in which they will be wet and cold tell them in advance. Halfway through a scene is no place to start haggling about fees and working conditions. Scenes of simulated sexual intercourse count as arduous work and additional discomfort.

Children

It is traditional and sound advice that actors should never work with children or animals. In view of some of the legal complexities producers and directors often come to feel the same way. Employing children invariably raises problems.

You may not make any use whatsoever of children under the age of sixteen in any type of production without the clear permission of their parent or lawful guardian. Life would be simple if that were the only restriction, but it is not. There are two areas of restriction on the use of children; those of general application and those specifically applicable to the contracting of children as performers. As a general point even if you only want to film documentary or interview children during their leisure or holiday time, whether in a public place or on private premises, you must have a licensed chaperone, parent, guardian, or someone in *loco parentis*, at all times. You cannot interfere with the education of a child. So you cannot ask for them to miss a day of school to accommodate your shooting requirements. You may ask permission to film on school premises and in normal hours but the teachers must weigh the benefits against the potential academic disruption.

Many schools, particularly primary ones, will be happy to receive crews, particularly if they see the programme to be in a good cause or can use the visit as an educational experience in itself. Many teachers, as well as children, love to see themselves on television and the offer of a tape of the rushes or the final production will almost always win friends. If you are producing a feature story about the school itself or teaching methods you will almost certainly be made welcome. If however you want to use the schoolchildren for humorous purposes, or as a background to your reporter or actors then you will probably be restricted to scheduled playtimes or time at the end of the school day. If you just want to use the school as a dramatic or picturesque location you will probably be told to go away and return in a holiday period or weekend after negotiating a facility fee and clearly spelling out how many children are to be employed.

In most private schools, and many local education authorities, the decision will be left to the head teacher, although there may have to be a reference to the chairman of the governors. However some local education authorities insist that applications to shoot on their premises go through a press or public relations department. This may involve a detailed correspondence, certainly the signing of indemnities, and even agreeing to editorial conditions. Give the wheels of bureaucracy time to turn. Even where the head teacher is empowered to make the decision he or she ought to give notice to the parents of the children involved, usually by sending a note home with them. If any parent then wishes to object to their particular child appearing on camera they may do so. You are not entitled to ask children or staff, including caretaking staff, to remain behind after normal hours and you may not specifically ask teachers to curtail or re-arrange lessons on your behalf. In the past few years local education authority schools have been encouraged to 'opt out' of local control, whilst those which remain under local council control have been obliged to take devolved control over their finances. This will have implications for television producers in establishing whether the head teachers, the governors, the local authority, or even the Department of Education and Science is calling the shots. And increasingly fees will no longer be limited to a free cassette or a small contribution towards the school film society.

The use of educational premises out of normal teaching hours or during the holidays is a different matter. Under these circumstances it must be assumed that you are only interested in the premises as a location. Schools of architectural interest or in picturesque surroundings are sought after by film and television companies and can provide an important source of income, so you will have to negotiate location facility fees. If you want to include children in your shooting, whether they come from outside or are from the school itself, you will be deemed to be employing them as performers. In this case no parent or teacher can give you a free hand. The law is laid down by the Home Office.

All children of under statutory school leaving age being employed on camera or on stage must be issued with a Home Office Licence issued through the local Licensing Authority. The only regular exception is that you may shoot a performance or rehearsals given by the school itself or by a club or youth organization as part of its normal activities, so long as no payment shall be given to the individuals taking part. The rules may be waived also for individuals conditional upon the child concerned having taken part in no sort of paid performance for more than three days in the previous six months, that there is no interference with schooling, and that the engagement is within the statutory maximum hours for the age of the child.

Children at stage schools are allowed slightly greater latitude and principals of such schools are very aware of the restrictions and can sometimes take the problems of licensing off your hands.

Conditions of employment depend upon age. At one extreme children under two may only work for a maximum of twenty minutes at a time with a maximum of one hour total per day and the working day must be between 9.30am and 4pm. From two to five year olds the period of performance is increased to thirty minutes with a two hours per day maximum and for five to nine year olds the allotted time increase to forty-five minutes and three hours respectively. Ten to twelve years old have the same maximum hours but the working day may be between 9am and 5pm. Only thirteen to sixteen year olds may be on set between 9am to 7pm and may be asked to work for periods of one continuous hour up to a maximum of three and a half hours per day. There is no distinction made between hours spent in rehearsal or in actual performance, and if children are expected to be at the studio or location for six hours or more they must have a scheduled hour and a half break between equal half sessions.

Even when children reach sixteen, as defined as the end of the term after their sixteenth birthday, they must still have the written permission of their head teacher if they wish to work during term time and are still in full time education.

Children work a five day week only. The maximum number of days any child may work is forty days in one year for under thirteens and eighty for over thirteens. Children are expected to continue their normal education during the maximum hours allocated for attendance on location or in studio. You have to be prepared to set aside special accommodation for the child, the chaperone, and possibly teachers as well.

The licensing authority is usually the local education authority. A licence may be refused if a completed application is not received at least twenty one days before the first day of production. Each child has to be licensed individually and all applications have to be accompanied by two passport size photographs and a copy of the child's birth certificate. The licence is contingent upon all the conditions specified above and may stipulate the tuition to be provided during the periods of the day not taken up by rehearsals or performance. If a parent or guardian is not present at all times the production company has to employ a full time chaperone or matron who must also be licensed. This applies even if the child is actually the son or daughter of one of the performers or your production team. You don't automatically get off the hook by asking your PA or cameraman to bring along their own kids for a part. Nor are you allowed to leave the supervision of children between takes to a kind wardrobe assistant or the office tea lady. They do not count as chaperones. Nor, if some parents or guardians are present, may you ask them to supervise other people's children.

This sounds horrifying, and actually it is. The total regulations are more complex than this brief résumé, and if you plan anything out of the ordinary, like going abroad, the magistrates may be involved. It is not worth trying to cut corners. If you do not keep strictly to the Home Office regulations you are automatically liable to prosecution. Locations employing children can be, and regularly are, paid surprise visits by inspectors. As a consequence every production is obliged to keep detailed records of each child's daily work sheet including arrival and departure times, hours of work, rest and meal breaks, periods of tuition, and so on. Failure to keep such records up to date and to produce them on demand is an offence. It can mean immediate withdrawal of licences and criminal prosecution for the production company.

Animals

Animals are as awkward as children to work with, and if they don't complain so much themselves they have plenty of people to complain on their behalf.

The legal situation is comparatively simple. Filming animals for documentary purposes in their natural environments should not cause many problems, however a great many natural history sequences are set up in anything but natural circumstances. Fortunately television has a way of causing the audience to suspend disbelief, and people no more question how a camera chanced to be around when a particular predator murdered its prey, than they query how the first man ever to conquer a mountain arrived in the shot of a camera which somehow got there first.

Natural history cameramen are jealous guardians of their techniques both to keep tricks of the trade from rivals, and to avoid criticism from animal welfare activists. So there are times when there is a risk of contravening cruelty to animals legislation. Live trapping animals or mist netting birds by experts risks a percentage of deaths or injuries, and even the use of live baits in fishing programmes can arouse protest. A problem is that a constructed animal sequence, like any other, demands repeated actions and set up cutaway shots. You must ask how many times you should return a hooked fish to the water or how far to risk distress to a nesting bird whilst getting your shot.

If your production clearly involves deliberately distressing animals for the camera then you risk committing a criminal offence. The likelihood of prosecution and the attitude of the animal protection societies will depend in part on contemporary public sensibilities, and certainly laboratories using animal experiments, even though licensed by the Home Office, have been forced to greatly restrict and modify their use of animals in recent years.

One consequence has been that many scientists who work with animals, even for simple psychological tests in a laboratory or on populations in the field, are very reluctant to be shown doing their work. It is always worthwhile clearing up in advance what will or will not be shown. Reactions may sometimes seem extreme. For example, one shoot involved a marine biologist investigating the decline of flatfish in the English Channel by taking the catch from the trawl and marking fish with a liquid nitrogen brand for later identification. Although the procedure apparently caused no distress and the victims were being spared the fishmonger's slab, the biologist refused, in mid ocean, to allow the fish to be filmed. He feared assault by extremist vegetarian groups. In this case the story was ruined and a disgruntled crew had to be bought off with a meal at a seafood restaurant.

However, there are some activities which can be in no way considered a matter for individual sensibilities. Do not get involved, even as an observer, in dog-fighting, badger digging, gin trapping or any other quaint and clearly illegal rustic pursuit. You will be prosecuted as an accessory to a criminal act.

Also remember that the list of protected species is long and ranges from the golden eagle to the humble newt. You may have to seek the permission of the Ministry of Agriculture or the Home Office for any shooting which might involve disturbance, and you will require the express permission of the landowners of any location. The Royal Society for the Prevention of Cruelty to Animals (RSPCA) or Royal Society for the Protection of Birds (RSPB) can advise you.

Shooting on the premises of zoos or wildlife parks might seem to be a solution. Alas cameras seem to have the same weird effect upon animals as they have on some humans. Any old television hand can recount tales of comatose cobras brought to life by a light, incontinent elephants, sex-maddened ducks, and escapologist apes. All animals are not equal. They come in three classes; dangerous animals, performing animals, and animals for demonstration.

Dangerous animals are defined by the Dangerous Wild Animals Act 1976. Under the Act there is a schedule of beasts which must be licensed by an owner or animal dealer. The function of the Act is not just to protect the animals but to protect the public from the sort of person who breeds rattlesnakes in the bath or uses a leopard as a fashion accessory. Dangerous animals must only be used with their licensed handlers and if there is any conceivable risk to technical crews, performers, or members of the public the advice of the RSPCA or qualified veterinary authorities should be sought. In the case of large dangerous animals a qualified vet equipped with the wherewithal to tranquillize or restrain the animal should be present.

Performing animals are normally domestic species or captive-bred animals and, since the virtual extinction of stage and circus animal performances these are generally supplied by agencies specializing in film and television work. All such agencies should be able to confirm in writing that their training methods have been in compliance with the Performing Animals Regulation Act 1925. Such animals will be supplied and transported by their own handlers who will also take responsibility for their welfare on location. It will however be up to you to make available access to water, shade, bedding and rest for the animals involved and to take advice on the length of time the creatures should be in front of the cameras and what periods of exercise and feeding are needed. Be prepared for the shots to take time. Animals only perform when they want to.

Animals for demonstration are those which are normally brought by their owners and range from a small boy showing off his pet gerbil through a shepherd and his dog, to a zoologist with a cage full of monkeys. In each of these cases you contract the owner or demonstrator who is responsible for the animals' welfare. This may seem simple but there is a tangle of additional regulations and innumerable eventualities which can make filming difficult.

During outbreaks of disease animals may become subject to Ministry of Agriculture movement restrictions. Pigs in particular may be subject to movement orders even without a swine fever outbreak in your locality. Straw on a set must be fire proofed without the fireproofing being toxic to the animals. Your performers and crew members must be consulted in advance. There are people who are wildly allergic to the fur of cats or become hysterical at the proximity of snakes or spiders.

Be very careful about using exotic species. The Convention on the International Trade in Endangered Species (CITES) prohibits the import of an enormous range of animals and animal products. There is, for example, a hugely lucrative trade in birds of prey and in many rare parrots. Such birds should be properly ringed as captive bred animals. The tightening of regulations may expose new grey areas. If it is now illegal for an unlicensed, unqualified beach photographer to use a monkey as a property, will it be similarly an offence for an actor to handle such an animal as part of a drama?

However, do remember that any animal placed in the unnatural environment of a television studio or film set can become a danger not just to others but to itself.

If your use of any category of animal might be intepreted as an animal performance you should give notification to the Veterinary Officer of your local government authority who has the right to visit and inspect. If you are going to shoot a sequence giving the illusion of cruelty you must notify the veterinary officer. You will know how to create the illusion of a horribly convincing dog fighting or animal maltreatment sequence through clever camera angles and creative editing. The measure of your success might be an investigation with a view to prosecution under the Protection of Animals Act 1911. The Act and subsequent amendments makes it illegal to broadcast programmes which show or have contributed to the maltreatment or distress of animals, whether or not the origination of the programme is from overseas. This could raise interesting problems. It is illegal in the UK to broadcast bullfighting, for example, although bullfighting scenes as part of a documentary programme would be acceptable so long as they were used for illustrative purposes. The production would in no way have been accessories to the cruelty any more than a war correspondent should have been an accessory to the atrocities he reports.

It will be interesting to see whether it will be illegal for Spanish television, which devotes many hours to bullfighting to be shown by subscription services on cable or satellite, after the abolition of internal frontiers within the EEC at the end of 1992. This question has already arisen over the broadcast of hard porn programmes by satellite from the Netherlands and Denmark which may be received on subscription channels in the United Kingdom.

The armourer

Any firearm or anything capable of launching a projectile must be considered as a potentially lethal weapon. So up to a point must any sword, knife or club in the hands of an actor whether or not it is a theatrical fake. When you are planning a fight sequence, or a hold-up scene, start thinking about whether you need to employ specialists. You may need specialist stuntmen and a specialist fight arranger. You will probably need an armourer even if shots are not to be fired or actual blows struck in vision.

If you are going to use firearms they must be in the hands of someone with the appropriate firearms licence or a registered arms dealer. There are several different licences. The most common is a simple shotgun licence which is easily obtained from the local police. If you want to prime the pan of an antique musket you will need a black powder licence, something which all special effects designers as well as armourers should possess. For handling rifled weapons, which includes almost all hand guns, apart from most air pistols, you will need to possess a firearms certificate which will be given by the police on receipt of *bone fide* reasons for possession being provided and specific obligations on the storage and security of the weapons and ammunition being maintained. Finally there is a Home Office Section Five Permit which allows the permit holder to handle weapons capable of automatic continuous fire. This is extremely difficult to obtain, and if you are hiring automatic weapons you must, at the outset, make sure that your supplier can legally offer the types of armament you require.

The above regulations apply whether you are using blanks or live ammunition. Only antique weapons used exclusively as ornaments and airguns of a specified low muzzle velocity do not need licences under current law.

If you have any doubts refer to the Firearms Act 1968 and consult the crime prevention officer at your local police station.

With fully practical firearms you must employ a qualified armourer who will conform with strict legal obligations concerning the transportation of the weapons and ammunition and supervise their use and security on location. Even apparently safe weapons can be lethal or disfiguring. Blank cartridges at close range can fire burning powder grains and blinding fragments of wadding or case. The British Armed Forces require a safe distance of thirty metres when blank ammunition is being used. This should be adhered to as far as possible using clever direction and sensible editing, but if the gunslinger and the victim have to appear in shot simultaneously as the trigger is pulled be *very* careful. Performers may never have handled a weapon before. They should never, never be allowed to point weapons directly at each other and the director or armourer should make sure that they understand completely how to convincingly 'aim off'. All weapons should be checked before and immediately after each take. This applies just as much to weapons which do not require a licence like airguns and bows and arrows. Treat crossbows as you would a rifle.

If you are planning a 'West Side Story' sort of production be aware that there is a schedule of prohibited weapons which are illegal to be imported or possessed, including flick knives and knuckledusters. On the stage you can get away with specially constructed harmless dummies, but on the small screen you will need close ups of the real articles and only an armourer is likely to be licensed to provide them. There is a vague area left by the Criminal Justice Act covering the theatrical uses of real swordsticks or types of martial arts weapons which in ordinary circumstances would be illegal in public. Your supplier will be able to advise if such weapons need the supervision of a qualified armourer or not.

It is easy to underestimate the lethal capacity of performers both amateur and professional. Buttons can come off the ends of fencing foils. Sharp edged weapons ought to be well blunted but a swashbuckling swordfight with blades clashed together edge to edge can result in them looking like sawblades. You need someone standing by to examine the swords between takes and attend to them with a grindstone or a file and hammer. This is another good reason for hiring your armament from a theatrical supplier. You may well be able to hire or borrow certain types of weapon from a private collector or antiques dealer but they will expect them to be returned in the condition you borrowed them. Your armourer will also be able to advise on whether the rental of arms includes other props and items of costume like scabbards, pistol cases, sword belts, holsters and so on. You need to be sure that you don't finish up hiring these items from a costumier and finding out that you are paying twice over.

Whenever you are using weapons on location where you may be seen by the public you must inform the local police. Firearms may not be carried openly in a public place or on or adjacent to public highways, even lanes in the heart of the countryside, so shotguns and even air rifles need a carrying case. Never underestimate the gullibility of the public. What is to you an obviously faked comic fight in a park can still result in a panic telephone call to the police from a passer by or the inhabitant of a distant block of flats. If you want to fire blanks, let alone live ammunition, you are going to need a suitably remote location such as a quarry, and if you want a battle it is advisable to hire the Ministry of Defence firing ranges.

If you can get away with using inoperative fake weapons there are great cost advantages. Moreover an actor is less likely to do any damage with a wooden or rubber copy than with the real thing. You must still be careful about the use of replicas in public places. In law a hold-up with a toy gun is the same as a hold-up with the proper item. Fake or real sawn-off shotguns are strictly illegal. If you want close-ups of desperate hand to hand combat you might be advised to get replica weapons cast in foam as an insurance against your performers knocking each others' teeth out.

The costs of hiring weapons is infinitely variable depending on the size, market value and scarcity. It can pay to shop around. The armourers will probably calculate charges at around 10 or 15% of replacement value but there may be one supplier who has acquired large stocks of, for example, old Lee Enfield rifles during past war story productions and will willingly rent these at knockdown prices. Some firms of armourers hold their own stocks of the most commonly demanded weapons, but many do not and have to hire from the larger suppliers. There is no central organization or agency for armourers. In London the largest supplier is probably Bapty's. Military firearms in particular are expensive. Something as common as a Russian AK47 rifle may set you back £40 per week at the time of writing, with the fees and expenses of the armourer and the costs of ammunition on top.

If you are in an area where there are no armourers, and your needs are simple, you can look through the local yellow pages for arms dealers. Many of these will do theatrical hiring. Your regional television company may inform you about local arms dealers they consider reliable. You must resist the temptation to cut costs by signing on some gun enthusiast from an amateur shooting club or even a properly licensed owner of the town gun and fishing tackle shop who nonetheless lacks any kind of television of theatrical experience. Employing a properly qualified armourer with appropriately supervised weaponry may drain your budget but will keep you and your production team out of jail and hospital.

Stuntmen

If you are planning any violent action sequences or are using potentially hazardous special effects you ought to think about employing stuntmen. Under no circumstances should you listen to the siren voices of amateurs, whether members of the unit or untrained cowboys who are eager to 'have a go' in front of the camera. A racing driver is not a stunt driver, and a famous rock climber is not to be trusted with a re-enactment of a struggle on the castle battlements. Not only are untrained stunt performers likely to kill themselves but they are a menace to other members of the cast and crew as well as the public at large. Your insurance cover may become void if you recklessly undertake stunts and your crew or cast will be entitled to refuse to work with non-professionals. Under the Health and Safety at Work Act you may be individually liable to criminal prosecution if anything goes wrong, in addition to the likelihood of a civil case for damages.

Danger apart there are good production reasons for hiring stuntmen. Currently the list of qualifications for stuntmen is being expanded to include proficiency in ordinary popular sports. It may be cheaper to sign on a bunch of professional athletes or squash players or world class rowers but that is to miss the point. A stuntman is a performer who is trained to depict certain physical skills. A sportsman is simply an athlete and unless you are very lucky the chance of turning one into an instant actor is almost zero. Stuntmen are highly experienced in the tricks of camera angles and the use of lenses and will be able to advise the less experienced director how to cheat moves to heighten the illusions of danger and suspense. Stuntmen are trained in illusion. They are trained specifically not to take risks. They will design and execute the most spectacular tricks for you only when they have made them completely safe. Macho actors may like to quote famous cinema performers from Buster Keaton onwards who insisted on doing their own stunts. A closer investigation of how much time some of these spent off work with broken bones is informative. The use of stunt doubles is money well spent.

All qualified stuntmen carry their own personal insurance arranged through Actors' Equity. This is in addition to the obligatory third party insurance which all productions take.

Entry into the ranks of stunt performers is strictly controlled. Entry is open to members of Equity aged between eighteen and thirty who may apply for a two year probationary membership. During this period they may act only as assistant to a stunt performer and cannot arrange or perform any stunt unsupervised. They must already be able to prove proficiency in at least six activities ranging from fencing to parachuting. After the probationary period the performer must spend a qualifying three years during which they may perform stunts so long as these entail danger to nobody but themselves. Only after this time may they arrange or perform in sequences which might put at risk other stuntmen or members of the unit.

Very experienced stunt performers often rise to style themselves stunt co-ordinators, fight arrangers, or second unit directors and are entrusted with the overall production of action sequences in large television programmes or feature films. Reputations circulate very much by word of mouth. Inevitably stunt performers work very closely with special effects designers and each may have their favourites, or horrors, in the ranks of the others.

The term stuntmen may be taken to include the large number of stunt women. As a choice of stunt doubles will depend upon both appearance and specific physical skills, advice on casting should be sought from the Equity Stunt Performers' Registry. Many actors and actresses advertise specific skills generally such as fencing and horse riding in the pages of *Spotlight*. You need to discuss with them exactly what is entailed, and how proficient they are before discarding the idea of stunt performers. Your performers may be skilled amateur swordsmen but it may still need a fight co-ordinator to choreograph the excitement you require.

Special effects designers

Special effects are not only commonly needed by drama productions, but are frequently required for many other programme areas including educational and childrens' programmes.

There are a whole range of fairly harmless rain, frost and smoke effects which a production might try on a do-it-yourself basis, assuming that your makeup supervisor, stage manager, scenic designer or whoever is willing and able. But for anything involving shattering objects, flames, floods or pyrotechnics you will need to employ a special effects designer.

Special effects, whether used in conjunction with stunt performers or not, are meant to look dangerous and very often are. So, as with the use of an armourer or stunt performer, this is an area where the enthusiastic amateur should be avoided like the plague. Into this category must be consigned many performers of the variety stage or circus who may perform well-rehearsed tricks with hoops of fire and the like in their own environment, but who can be a danger in the very different circumstances of a film or television shoot. On the other hand until recently there was no common register or qualification for effects designers. Effects men tended to drift into their business from many other areas of the industry and pick up the tricks of the trade, generally working for large companies, as they went along. Effects designers are inspired improvisers and reputations have been made very much by word of mouth. The credibility of many an action sequence is the work of the effects designer. Many cameramen on the other hand regard them collectively as homicidal pyromaniacs and work on the principle that the effects man gives a safe distance for the camera which you then double and add twenty yards. Both cameramen and scenic designers, to whom the effects designers frequently work, will know which effects designers they trust to create the required effects without too many tears.

Since 1988 there has been a register of special effects technicians set up by the Independent Film and Television Producers Association and the Independent Programme Producers Association, now amalgamated as the Producers' Alliance for Cinema and Television (PACT), and administered by BECTU. There is a lengthy career ladder starting with five years as a trainee and another five as a technician working as part of a team. Only as a Senior Technician or, at least five years on, as a fully qualified Special Effects Supervisor can special effects be created and executed.

But there are still excellent and experienced specialists in fields like pyrotechnics who as yet have not joined the register. A fully qualified designer/supervisor is expected to be familiar not only with the traditional mechanical effects and explosions but to know about electronic and electrical controls, model effects, miniatures, and post-production techniques. The new world of digital effects which incorporate live action, models, digitally manipulated artwork, and so on, may be producing visual effects designers a long way from the exploding-car-man-thrown-through-window whizzbangery of yesteryear.

In the meantime you should make sure to employ a reputable company and consult it early on in your production planning. Special effects may well determine the shooting schedule for the whole production and ideally the special effects designer should attend even early recces of locations.

CHAPTER 5

Health and safety

Harold Lloyd in *Safety Last*, 1923. © CCN – Eastern Hemisphere 1923 (1950). All rights reserved. Still provided by the British Film Institute.

As a member of a television company you are covered by the same Health and Safety at Work Act as all other employers and employees. Studios are as much industrial premises as biscuit factories and are subject to all the laws, by-laws and regulations which cover everything from the provision of fire exits to the supply of soap in the lavatories.

Employer's responsibilities

The onus for the welfare of employees is placed squarely on the shoulders of the employers. Large companies employ full time safety officers and smaller ones nominate an employee to act in this capacity. On a location the person directing is usually responsible, although on a larger shoot where there is a production manager it may be he who carries the can. With multicamera electronic studios or outside broadcasts responsibility may be split between the production manager or floor manager who is responsible for safety on the actual set and a chief engineer who is responsible for other safety precautions.

Most of the time health and safety rules should not impinge on the work of the programme maker although personal clashes over interpretation between zealous fire or security officers and programme directors are not unheard of. Problems are most likely to arise on location where there is no safety supervision and there is a producer desperate to avoid an over-run, a director behind schedule or a reporter eager to demonstrate his journalistic machismo. This leads to the inevitable temptation to turn a blind eye to the rules and take risky on-the-spot decisions. There is a gamblers' side to most creative people. But when a gamble misfires and someone gets hurt matters will not end with an out-of-court insurance settlement. A culprit will be found and the result will not only be a claim for damages in the civil courts but possible criminal prosecution for negligence.

That said the law does take into account the custom and practice of the industry in defining which actions are reasonable and which are not, and how responsibility may be apportioned. For example, it will be understood that a news cameraman will be likely, as part of his normal duties, to place himself in situations of risk which would not be appropriate to the customary working practices of a shop assistant. But if he is sent to sea without a life jacket or is asked to climb a steeple without a safety line, the director or editor responsible is in breach of the law and liable for the consequences. Detailed safety regulations can, and do, fill books. Some details, such as those covering fire lanes are very specific, whilst common sense should alert you to most of the others.

Employers are legally obliged to make their employees aware of health and safety and there is no defence in the appeals of 'They should have known' or 'Nobody told me'. At the very least, everyone in the industry ought to have spent some time going through the relevant regulations and there should always be someone designated to check the rules and act as a point of reference. Whether you are a young local reporter telling a cameraman without a helmet to take a shot from a motorcycle pillion, or the production manager re-staging the Battle of Alamein, your main areas of responsibility are as follows.

1. You are responsible for the safety and maintenance of all equipment whether a prop gas fire or a studio gallery.
2. You are responsible for the handling and storing of all articles and substances used on a production. This is obvious when you are talking about pyrotechnics and firearms but there are less well known hazards. Stage cosmetics often include in their composition highly flammable solvents, glues and acetone. Never put an oil heater in an unventilated improvized make-up area on a winter location. You are responsible for training and supervising your personnel.
3. You are responsible for ensuring easy access and maintaining clear emergency exit routes. Never block entrances or emergency exits with vehicles or equipment. The incorrect positioning of lights in corridors or on staircases can be hazardous. Even if you are in a hurry to set things up on location it always pays to find out who the local fire officer/safety officer is and to get his agreement for what you plan to do. Cables create most problems. Carry heavy duty adhesive tape to fix loose cables down and never leave lights on stands unattended or attached to a cable running over ground which people might cross.
4. You are responsible for the general health and welfare of your personnel. This means you shall not demand they work in conditions of inadequate heating, lighting or ventilation. You are responsible for the provision of proper first aid equipment, washing facilities and lavatories.
5. You are responsible for the safety inspection of equipment. Studio hoists must be regularly inspected and certificates issued at the time. Camera cranes and studio mountings must be inspected and certificated for specific payloads and safety of hydraulics. Both private and commercial vehicles are liable to Ministry of Transport regulation and inspection. You remain liable, even at second hand, for airworthiness and seaworthyness of craft hired for a production.

6. You are responsible for employing only qualified personnel. If you stage a stunt it is up to you to check the qualifications of your stunt performer in the stunt register. The same applies to aircraft pilots, boat skippers and drivers. If you let some enthusiastic 'cowboy' act irresponsibly, or encourage an untrained member of the public to act dangerously, or ask an unsupervised member of your team to do something hazardous beyond their normal duties, there is no defence in claiming 'He said he wanted to do it.'
7. You are responsible for proper communications and proper rehearsals. An awful lot of the most serious accidents in film and television have happened because fights or stunts were not properly rehearsed with everyone involved present, or where someone has had a bright idea at the last moment and changed the action without communicating it to every single member of the team.
8. You are responsible for taking the specific precautions which are involved in filming at night near railways, roadways or docksides and for liaising with the appropriate police, safety and rescue authorities. Dazzling lights are a known hazard to people at a distance who have nothing to do with your shoot.
9. You are responsible for the provision of all appropriate safety equipment such as hard hats, life jackets, seat belts, safety lines, glasses, ear defenders, footwear and so on.
10. You are responsible for the inspection of all stairs, ladders, scaffolding, rostra and anything which will have to take the payload of crew, performers or equipment. This applies equally to the rickety bell tower of an ancient church or to a specially constructed audience seating area.

Within these ten guidelines the list of elaborations is almost infinite. To give a couple of examples, all sets and costumes should be adequately fire-proofed and you must check with rental companies that this is so. It is easy to be tempted, when working with outsiders not to check that their own costumes and properties have been treated. An easy oversight is the requirement for fireproof hairpieces. Real hair wigs are safe but enormously expensive to hire. You can get cheap artificial fibre ones from any joke shop, but some of them may be positively dangerous on set if not sprayed with fire retardant.

New problems keep arising. Water pollution has become a major health hazard so if you are going to take your personnel on or into doubtful waters it is up to you to have samples taken. The National Rivers Authority or local Environmental Health Officers should be able to advise, but you may have to arrange for specialist samples – alas, today even for offshore waters. Results may be received in a week although some very specialized analyses may take up to six weeks. Some waterways, although heavily used by pleasure craft, are now badly infected with Weil's disease which is spread by rats and you may find cameramen unwilling to get in contact with the water. They have the right to refuse even if you regard this as excessively fastidious. If in doubt seek advice from the responsible environmental agency and, if appropriate, also seek medical advice.

Insurance

Things that can go wrong invariably do so. The answer is to be properly insured against the consequences. If you are the full time employee of one of the large broadcasting companies you ought to be insured for all activities undertaken on their behalf. This doesn't mean that such insurance meets your personal needs. Cover for accidental death or injury whilst at work or travelling may be not generous and a wise employee might be advised to increase his personal cover. Most large companies will give life cover to its employees whilst travelling by air but refuse to be responsible for personal baggage loss. The problem has become complicated by the steady conversion of the broadcasting companies to becoming publishers rather than initiators of programmes.

The broadcasting companies will give independent productions their set of guidelines for insurance, but it is up to the independent companies themselves to negotiate their policies and it is they, not the broadcasting company, who are responsible. However the budget negotiated between the producer and the commissioning body should take account of the costs of insurance. For an absolute minimum cover you are advised to calculate at 1% of your gross budget, but for insurance against all eventualities the figure rises to 3% or over. Cover should be calculated from the first working day of pre-production to the date at which the last contracted member of staff is off the payroll. In cases where insurance against defamation or breach of copyright may arise it is advisable to maintain some insurance for several years thereafter.

As with everything else the extent of the cover you choose will depend on the scale and complexity of your production. But whether you represent the local film society, are making a few pennies at a wedding, or remaking *Ben Hur*, you must have appropriate cover. Insurance comes under six main categories.

1. Employers Liability
   This is obligatory under the Employers Liability Compulsory Insurance Act 1969. It must cover all employees of a production whether salaried or freelance, full time or briefly connected in any way. It must cover death, injury and illness as a result of work and is for unlimited liability. For a claim to succeed the employer has to be shown negligent.
2. Public Liability
   This is not obligatory but a company would be unwise not to take out such cover. The frequently quoted minimum cover is for £1 million. Many organizations or property owners will not allow you on site

without proof of public liability insurance. Such a policy will give as a minimum insurance against damage to property or injury to any third parties. The full extent of the indemnity will depend on the scale of the production and it is often advisable to extend cover to the use of motor vehicles involved in a production, both those specially hired and those personally owned.

3. Negative Insurance
   This offers additional cover particularly for extended productions involving contracted artists. It covers the costs of a re-shoot due to mechanical breakdowns, faulty film stock etc.
4. All Risk Equipment and Properties
   Some companies own much of their own equipment, and have to decide how much they can afford for normal commercial insurance against fire, theft, and accident. But most productions hire equipment, costumes, sets and properties. The production is usually responsible from the moment when it takes acceptance of such material to the moment when it is safely returned according to the rental agreement. Do not be over optimistic about the generosity of rental terms. Costume hire will often attract a hefty penalty where items are returned stained or with missing buttons. Obvious damage to properties or costumes may result in a bill for replacement.
5. Errors and Omissions
   This is cover against the risk of civil action by third parties for infringement of copyright, trespass or libel.
6. Union Insurance
   These are terms of insurance agreed between the main commissioning companies and the main trades unions. These cover responsibility for health, safety, accident and personal effects whenever you take a hired crew abroad. Similar cover may be required for work involving shooting at sea, on aircraft, on mountains or involving stunts or special effects. Both technicians and performers may refuse to work without evidence of such insurance cover.

There are as usual almost unlimited other factors for which you might need to insure.

You can insure against:

- the weather
- mechanical breakdown
- unreliability of star performers
- animals
- aircraft
- underwater sequences

- hi-jack, kidnap, ransom, and political upheaval.

If in doubt find an insurance broker who has experience in these and other matters.

CHAPTER 6

Copyright

Copyright is the body of law which protects authors of original works from the unlicensed pirating of their labours by others. 'If it's worth copying, it's worth protecting'.

Anyone working in television needs to be aware of the copyright which he or she can own in their own work, as well as the rights which may be assigned to others. Copyright can easily be infringed through ignorance and carelessness. The detailed interpretation of copyright is fiendishly complicated and what follows should only be taken as an outline of the main problems. Suffice to say that if you fall foul of copyright laws you can be in for a very expensive legal experience.

A typical television programme may involve a registered format, written screenplays or commentary scripts, live performances, live and recorded music, still photographs, quotations from previous works, illustrative archive film or video clips and much more besides. Each contribution to the final work may be subject to individual copyright and each of these copyrights may themselves be complicated.

In the case of a piece of recorded music for example, a whole complexity of copyright exists involving composers, performers, arrangers, publishers and record manufacturers.

The recognition of copyright is the very basis for the complex network of fees, residual revenues and contractual agreements on which our industry is based. In the world of television almost every creative participant is at some point an author as well as an exploiter of copyright materials. Anything from the title of a work to the typeface used by a graphic designer or an item of computer software may be subject to copyright. An author is anyone who produces original work. The term includes writers, composers, photographers, designers, musicians, actors, choreographers etc. Each contributor may have personal rights in the films, books, recordings or television programmes to which their original contributions are only a part.

The issue is further complicated because there may be secondary rights in completed works. For example a television broadcasting company or a publisher may have rights over a complete broadcast programme in addition to the individual copyrights of those authors who contributed to making it. In the same way a book publisher holds the copyright to an anthology of poems whilst each contributing poet maintains the copyright to the individual poem.

Generally copyright owners have the sole legal right to authorize the use of their own original work for any purpose whatever, and also hold a negative right, i.e. the author may prohibit you from making use of his work and take you to court if you use it without his authority.

Of course there will be occasions when establishing copyright becomes terribly difficult. Authors move or emigrate, publishing and television companies go out of business, authors die and you may have no way of tracing their heirs. In the comparatively simple area of the printed word your best insurance is to place an advertisement in an appropriate journal such as the *Times Literary Supplement* stating that you have exhausted all reasonable lines of enquiry and stating that you intend to publish unless further information is forthcoming. You will be further covered if you include words to the same effect in the acknowledgements section of your publicity and publication. However, technically you will still be in breach of the law and the author could still emerge to stop you using his work or to demand a fee. If the demands seem exorbitant the Society of Authors can advise on current standard charges and may advise you on how to deal with the problem.

There is no copyright in facts or news or information. But there is copyright in any arrangement or selection of the material which involves original labour. For example for many years the BBC's *Radio Times* and Independent Television's *TV Times* protected their exclusive publication of programme listings from competitors on copyright grounds until three days before transmission. Subsequent government intervention has obliged them to give up this monopoly but they are still able to invoke copyright to enforce payment from any paper publishing their programme schedules. The Football League similarly claims copyright in its list of match fixtures and demands royalties from the football pools promoters, although it chooses not to claim its rights in the case of newspapers or television sports programmes whose coverage they regard as valuable publicity.

There is no copyright in ideas. Documentary makers, in particular, are at risk because their programme subject proposals are often rejected by a broadcaster only to re-emerge later in near identical form under another producer. The only safeguard is to register any original idea as a fully worked out written treatment, so that if blatant plagiarism takes place, copyright in the treatment rather than the subject matter may be established. The 'Rock Follies' case, discussed below, illustrates this point.

Copyright law

It would be helpful if all copyright was governed by the same laws. Unfortunately this is not the case. Copyright is defined by successive acts, the Copyright Act 1911, the 1956 Copyright Act, and the Copyright,

Designs and Patents Act 1988 which became effective on 1 August 1989. Each Act does not entirely replace the previous one and most rights given by one act are not removed by subsequent ones. Copyrights established between 1911 and 1956 are subject to the old law, those between 1956 and 1989 by the later law and subsequent new copyrights are governed by the latest legislation.

Under the 1988 Act copyright in all literary, dramatic, musical or artistic works lasts for fifty years after the death of the author. Under the 1956 Act, works published after the death of an author became subject to copyright for fifty years after the first date of publication. This can create problems for biographers discovering unpublished manuscripts or television researchers using material from unpublished fifty-year-old diaries and correspondence.

Copyright in films, television programmes, or radio broadcasts dates from the first transmission or public showing for fifty years.

Copyright is automatically infringed if an original work is reproduced without permission. This includes publicly performing or rebroadcasting a work in part or in whole or publishing it for sale in recorded or printed form or copying it in any material way through sound or video recording or photocopying. All copying is not illegal but the exceptions tend to be specific. Educational bodies are subject to very special exemptions since educational broadcasts are clearly designed for subsequent re-use. It is accepted that a research student might photocopy original library material for presentation in a thesis although were the thesis subsequently to be published the material would be subject to copyright.

It seems to be acceptable to make a home video or sound recording of a programme originated and transmitted by the broadcast company. It is not at all certain whether copyright may be infringed if the object of the taping is a cinema feature film licensed to the broadcast company for a specific number of performances. Were the law to be tested to the finest detail it is likely that half the population would finish up in court.

You are certainly chancing your luck if you include previously broadcast or recorded material in any of your own productions without obtaining permission from the copyright owner – even for closed circuit or amateur club purposes. You will be in clear breach of the law if you include such material in any kind of paying performance or public presentation. The laws against commercial video piracy have been tightened and commercial piracy is a criminal offence attracting up to two years in jail and unlimited fines.

But small scale piracy, which is often unknowingly done, poses a problem which will not go away. New audio and video technology puts high calibre piracy within everyone's grasp. The new generation of digital equipment and high definition television will mean that any home will be able to make perfect unblemished copies of recordings from either transmission or purchased tapes. Solutions currently suggested include the outright ban on twin deck cassette machines, the insertion of spoiling systems on broadcast or pre-recorded discs and tapes and a levy on blank tapes or discs. In the same way publishers are concerned about the widespread use of high quality photocopying of books. The problems of computer program piracy are similar.

Television directors are likely to be both beneficiaries and exploiters of copyright problems and ought to be concerned that if technical innovations mean that uncontrolled copying cannot be stopped, at least a means for authors to derive an income from it should be found.

Photographs, art and design

All original art works, paintings, drawings and designs are subject to copyright. These may include brochures, dust jackets and even pub signs. Most fonts and typefaces are subject to copyright laws. All photographs published either in the press or on television are subject to copyright. All cartoon characters are copyright, and indeed the royalties from licensing the use of such characters often far exceeds any income derived from the original cartoons. Three dimensional objects together with their original designs are copyright, including original costumes, sculptures and stage sets or architectural models. So long as the object has entailed original work it may have copyright implications. The 1988 Act has in some ways simplified matters, but some differences in copyright remain, depending on the nature of the work concerned.

Copyright in original works under both the old and new acts extends for fifty years from the end of the calendar year in which the author died. There have been legal fights between copyright holders and companies who have assumed that the copyright expired at the beginning of the fiftieth year, and the publishing companies have had to make hefty payments to a dead author's estate. Copyright in original works still applies if such works are part of a larger entity. For example, an animated graphics title sequence to a programme will be the copyright of the artist unless his contract specifically assigns such copyright to the production company. Prints and engravings also remain in copyright for fifty years after the death of the author, but under the old law copyright in prints held in private collections after the death of an artist might become copyright from fifty years after the first publication.

Photographs are the subject with which the television director is most likely to be concerned, and each change in the law has created additional problems. Photographs are by their nature infinitely reproduceable and in many cases the circumstances and even the date of an original may be obscure. The 1911 Act dated fifty years copyright protection from the date on which the photograph was taken. Unfortunately many famous early photographs cannot be dated and indeed attribution may be in doubt. Time is slowly dealing with this problem. Under the 1957 Act copyright was dated for fifty years from the date of first publication or broadcast. This could mean that pictures taken from a hitherto private photograph album would begin a fifty year copyright protection from the moment of their first use, although they themselves were fifty years old. The 1988 Act brought photography into line with literary copyright, i.e. the photographer becomes the primary owner of the copyright in his work and protection lasts for fifty years from the death of the photographer.

This is fine so far as the amateur or completely speculative freelance photographer is concerned, but most photographers work to precise commissions for others, whether their specialities are wedding snaps, newspapers or advertisements. Under the 1956 Act the copyright of the picture was vested in the person who commissioned it, in other words whoever paid for the film in the camera retained the copyright of the images produced. This meant that photographs commissioned from either staff or freelance photographers by newspapers, television programmes or periodicals became automatically the copyright of those organizations, and this put photographers apart from writers and other creative artists. The new law gives copyright to he who presses the shutter button. It has been suggested that if you hand your camera to someone else to take your picture on holiday, the copyright belongs automatically to the stranger.

The commissioning organization will retain copyright on the photographs taken for the stated purpose of the commission, so a staff photographer of one newspaper may not sell such photographs to a rival, although a freelance shooting on spec may do so. But copyright in the use of such a photograph for other purposes, so long as they are not directly contrary to the interests of the original commissioner, remain with the photographer. As usual copyright may be assigned, and a photographer may contractually assign most rights to an employer. This means that when you come to the practical business of using a photograph in a television programme, even one which has already been published by others, the business of determining the true copyright holder is by no means simple. Was the photographer an employee and all rights assigned to the commissioning publication? Was he a freelance worker who retained certain rights contractually? Was the picture a private one or submitted on spec? Who owns the original negative?

Even an item as commonplace as a wedding photograph can be fraught with complications. If the photographer was specifically commissioned the copyright should be held by the happy couple. But if the photographer was an employee of the local press then the newspaper would hold the rights. If the photographer was a freelance copyright might be his, but he still should not use it without permission of the couple. If copyright belongs to the couple then copyright is owned jointly. You therefore need two permissions to be able to reproduce the pictures, even if the partners have subsequently divorced. Even if it is shot on spec the photograph may not be sold on for advertising purposes.

The 1988 Act introduced into English law for the first time the continental right of paternity in a work, expressed in the Act as an authors 'moral right'. The law aims to protect an original work from being unjustifiably altered or misused in a way detrimental to the work itself or its author's reputation. In France this moral right has been invoked by film directors to try to prevent television companies from interrupting full length features with obtrusive commercial breaks. In the USA there have been similar fights to prevent companies using digital effects technology to colour films originally shot in black and white. The test seems to be that the purchaser of a copyright may make alterations to an original work so long as it is 'reasonable in the circumstances and not detrimental to the honour and reputation' of the author. This, however, will not stop a picture editor cropping a photograph, nor will you be able to invoke moral right if your commissioning editor or senior producer tells you to cut out ten minutes of your favourite footage from a documentary. But if the finished work is subsequently re-edited for satirical purposes, or used in completely inappropriate advertising copy, the author might seek redress. There are no guidelines as to what may or may not be appropriate, nor clear indications of the sort of damages which might be awarded since, as with libel cases, we are dealing as much with wounded pride as quantifiable damage. Photographers and film or television directors are notoriously touchy about the use and abuse of their work, even where copyright belongs to others or where they believe that due credit has not been publicly given. This is an area of law to watch with interest. The new law also gives photographers, film and television directors (though not staff journalists or photographers), the right to a prominent credit on publication of their work.

The great majority of photographs and prints used in television are to be located in the two hundred and more British picture libraries which may contain general news pictures or specialist collections in subjects as diverse as theatrical prints, animals or space exploration.

Apart from supplying their own original material these libraries often act as agents for contributing freelance photographers. Original material ought to be supplied for a fee clear of subsequent copyright and the agency or library ought to have made its own arrangements but this may not be the case and you need to reassure yourselves that you have unqualified television rights. If the photograph you want can only be located in a published book or periodical, the publishers of which no longer exist or for whom you have no records, you must look for the attribution either alongside the picture or in the acknowledgement of picture sources at the beginning or end of the book. You must then make an effort to trace the copyright holder, even though you are only taking a picture of a picture. If the photograph is essential and there seems no way of locating the copyright holder, you could decide to take a chance and use it anyway, making sure that you credit the last known source and publish a disclaimer. If the original copyright holder then turns up, you can offer him a reasonable fee. He might still take you to court or seek to prevent any repeat use of his material. Taking you to court will not be a very profitable exercise as the award is unlikely to be greater than a reasonable fee to be expected under the circumstances but you are taking a grave risk. Don't assume that you can make use of published photographs willy-nilly in the hope that you will only get caught from time to time and will only have to pay minimal fees when you do. The courts will award damages as appropriate if you cannot show that you have taken every reasonable step to locate the copyright holder.

Portraits may raise a problem in that the subject may or may not have commissioned the photograph. If all is not clear it is only safe to get the consent for the use of a portrait from the sitter as well as the photographer. The use of portraits might also be an area to be complicated by the invocation of the novel idea of moral right, which could be invoked by either the photographer or his sitter. Libel laws might be invoked to prevent intrusion into private lives on the basis that the unwanted publication of a picture might constitute a breach of confidence between the portraitist and the sitter, even where the photographer retains copyright in the first instance. The publication of indecorous or indiscrete photographs during the lifetime of the subject could be grounds for legal action. The publishing of such pictures in a scandalous context is a regular problem for the tabloid press but ought to be less of a problem for the television director. Remember, there can be a moral right in the owners or subject of domestic photographs and home movies or videotapes. You must get clearance to use these.

Paintings which have been purchased for public collections and are on permanent display may usually be assumed to be free of copyright so long as they are outside the fifty year limits. A museum or gallery may hold works on loan or a contemporary artist might have contrived to retain reproduction rights in return for selling or donating his works. With photographs the problem is by its nature more acute since there may be more than one author's print exhibited in different collections. Opinion is divided about whether a photograph, film, or videotape of a work of art is in itself subject to copyright. As a rule of thumb a photograph of a picture on a wall is a simple reproduction and not subject to any new copyright, whereas a creatively lit interpretative shot of a sculpture or architectural detail might well be so.

You are not even completely home and dry with old masters. Rubens and van Gogh may no longer be able to collect on their work but museums are not likely to give you *carte blanche* to rush into their collections and start snapping away. For practical safety reasons photographic lights are forbidden in galleries. The use of tripods during public hours will not be allowed, and permission to shoot after hours, which would entail the disruption of security and staffing arrangements, may be unobtainable. Many museums, libraries and collections will only allow filming or photography under supervision in their own studios. There can be long waiting lists and high charges. To compensate, most works are held on high quality photographic transparencies and unless it is essential to set a presenter in an actual gallery context, the use of transparencies with rostrum camera work is the most effective and satisfying way to present artwork. But remember the galleries will charge for the supply and reproduction of such prints or transparencies, effectively retaining control over their use.

In recent years there has been an ever growing pressure on picture collections from television directors, and at the same time such collections, including small local collections, have been driven to seek profits. The days when a picture researcher could carry off files full of material to study at leisure, or spend bookish days in commercial collections browsing at no cost, are fond memories. Your picture research will entail a varying number and scale of fees.

Access fees are a sort of temporary reading room ticket charged if you wish to do your own research in a library. They are generally charged by public museums and archives. *Search fees* are payable when you commission the owners or librarians of a collection to search out specific stills for you. They can be very high so get an estimate before you begin. *Service fees* cover handling and the post and packing of pictures sent out. At the time of writing they are between £15 and £40. *Rental fees* are payable for the days during which you retain the pictures. Many libraries lend material free of rental for a limited period, but thereafter you pay fines, like those on unreturned public library books. Extensions are usually granted. After a period, frequently a short one, you may be deemed to have lost or taken the picture and the library will bill you for a replacement cost which will be fixed at a punitive level. You may well be charged several hundred pounds replacement cost for even quite unexceptional looking material. *Reproduction fees* are a licence to reproduce the pictures on paper, film or videotape. The supplying picture library may not be able to assign a total copyright licence if the material is not of its own origination. Finally there are *reference fees*: set designers, costume designers and graphic artists regularly need picture research for reference purposes but without the intention to directly copy the originals in any way. They will still be expected to pay an artist's reference fee. The temptation to cheat arises when the material is clearly too old to still attract copyright and exists as prints or photographs in old magazines or books. Several picture libraries may possess copies of the same material, so you could get a transparency of, for example, a 19th century cartoon and claim that the version you finally use came from some other source. The deviousness involved in trying to get out of part of a fee is hardly worth the effort. If you don't pay up the offended library will probably refuse to do business with you again.

Most picture libraries are now linked in the British Association of Picture Libraries which can advise on specialist collections. Note that the Crown reserves a special copyright. The Royal Family essentially has its own copyright and even shots of a ceremony such as the Coronation will need authorization by the Palace authorities. Banknotes, coins, postage stamps and maps originating from the Ordnance Survey are all covered by their own copyrights.

As with other laws, copyright applied to the last legal detail would make life quite impossible for the director. It would appear that a director might be liable to prosecution for including so much as a shop window display, advertisement poster, or magazine cover in a shot without having to clear all copyright first. To get around this the courts accept the concept of 'fair dealing'. You will be reckoned to have dealt fairly under certain limited circumstances. If the work shown is on regular public display you will be dealing fairly, so the statue in the park problem is solved. But this only applies if your portrayal is incidental to the main action. For example if you do an interview in front of a museum poster you are being fair as the picture is 'incidental', but if the poster is by a prominent modern artist and your designer deliberately incorporates it as a feature in a set for a drama you could be in trouble.

Artists and designers have their own copyright protection society. It is fair dealing to use material, written or graphic, to illustrate a critical programme or a review, although this does not entitle you to use copies of photographs. The percentage of a review which may be taken up with quotations is arguable, but authors and publishers have an interest in fighting to keep the percentage low. In quoting or illustrating you should always give prominent acknowledgement to the author, you should have come by the material fairly, and not use the material in such a way whereby your publication could in any way impinge upon the sales or other profits from the original. To use material for the purpose of reporting news or current affairs is legitimate and if there is an attempt to use copyright laws to block a report it is possible to appeal to the courts using the defence of public interest.

If you infringe copyright by accident and can prove that you had done your homework and honestly thought that a work was free of copyright the copyright owner cannot claim damages, although he can still claim a fee. Fair dealing is one of those slippery concepts which has been too little tested in court for good general legal advice to be available.

The new Act has extended to television images the same protection as still photographs so you may not copy an image off the screen or from a videotape without clearance. However there have been recent cases of broadcast television companies pirating each other's footage off transmission to include in their own news reports. So long as the original sources are acknowledged and the material used to illustrate an issue of the moment it is possible that a defence of either 'fair dealing' or 'public interest' might apply under the new Act. However, the copyright of a still photograph would be infringed if it were used for reporting current events without permission and prior agreement of a fee.

Film copyright

Documentary directors in particular frequently need to use news archive film or video material, or use extracts from dramatic television works or feature films.

A piece of film falls under the same rules as a stills photograph under the Copyright Act. Newsreel shots are covered for fifty years and subject to the same rules as newspaper photographs, i.e. the copyright may belong to the photographer or may have been assigned contractually to a commissioner. Moral rights apply. Feature films are further covered as dramatic works and are protected for fifty years from the death of the author.

At this point the problems begin. Who is the author of a collective enterprise like film? Is it the director, screenwriter, author of an adapted work, producer or star performer? Each and every one will have rights and these will be defined in the complex web of contracts surrounding a feature film production. The National Film Archive suggests that you are not certainly free of possible complications until you are sure that every single credited contributor to a feature is long dead and buried.

The 1958 Copyright Act tried to simplify the issue by assigning the copyright of film shot after 1958 to the Producer. Copyright commences with the start of shooting and then extends for fifty years from the first public showing. After fifty years the film should enter the public domain. This has been the case in the USA with the result that an ever increasing number of cinema classics are available.

But copyright can be bought and sold. In the volatile world of the film industry copyright may be contractually split and traded between producers, studios, performers, broadcasters and distributors. Cinema is also totally cosmopolitan. Copyright contracted in one country may not pertain to another. So you would be very unwise to look at the credits and assume that the producer possesses all the copyrights of all the contributors to his product, from the screenplay and the musical score to the special make-up.

So clearances for feature films are fiendishly complex and unless you have the support of a special administrative department to go into battle on your behalf it is best to assume that any feature or dramatic work under fifty years old is unclearable. Having said that, there are collections and libraries of material for which all rights have been cleared or have expired. If you are lucky and find what you need from such a source you need to reassure yourself in writing that your supplier takes responsibility. The supplier should guarantee that he owns all film and musical rights in the production. The supplier should indemnify you against any subsequent claim for breach of copyright. The supplier should also guarantee to supply material of appropriate technical quality, which means you will not be landed with a VHS cassette or a 16 mm print that has seen the rounds of a dozen film societies. As always you must contractually specify whether you want broadcast or home video sales or overseas rights and, if negotiating for broadcast, be clear about repeat payments. Unfortunately the suppliers may simply impose their own conditions and these can be infinitely variable. These may include a demand for a minimum royalty on loaning out material whether or not it is finally used in your production, a payment per foot supplied rather than per foot transmitted or used, or a refusal to accept responsibility for any residual payments. The only extracts you can approach with safety are publicity shots and trails issued for works currently on release and made conditionally available to boost cinema attendances or video sales. You have to make your own clearances. Remember that the owner of home video rights may not be the same as the owners of the theatrical rights or those to 16 mm copies.

Fees may also be infinitely variable. Much may, or may not, depend on the size and distribution of your production. To give an example, the fees paid for national transmission by the BBC in 1990 ranged from £650 per minute to Columbia Films or $4,000 per minute to Warner Brothers down to £5 per second transmitted for the Movietone Film Library or £5.50 per 35 mm foot for the Rank Organisation. The Imperial War Museum charged only £2.50 per 35 mm foot with a minimum order of thirty feet. MGM productions were regarded as unclearable.

Note that you may under no circumstances pirate copyright material transmitted on television, nor make use of any material available for sale or rental as home video. Film is also one of the few areas which is excluded from the copyright exemption given to genuine students or researchers. Even for a student project the use of uncleared material is illegal.

Although libraries increasingly hold copies on video cassettes this is not always so and you may have to have access to an editing bench. Film viewing can be an expensive business. Charges may vary depending on whether you do your own research, or whether you must use library staff to locate the required material and whether it is obligatory for them to be present to supervise a viewing.

A lot of material shot before the early 1950s is still on nitrate film stock. This is extremely volatile and can turn to explosive with age so viewing is subject to stringent safety restrictions. In a similar way many not so old television productions exist on videotape formats which are now obsolete and for which only a very few playback machines still exist. If you are operating on film you will probably need to order duplicate 16 mm negatives and prints from original 35 mm or even larger projection formats. Laboratory fees can be high – hence the rise of videotape over other formats. Nonetheless the cost of machine time to transfer cinema footage onto your chosen video format may not be cheap either.

CHAPTER 7

Music and musicians

Laurel & Hardy in *Saps at Sea*, 1940. Still provided by the British Film Institute.

In order to avoid an unpleasant shock when the music bills come in, the sensible independent producer will engage the services of an experienced musical director and union approved contractor. The musical director for the recording sessions may be the same person who composed the music but this is not always the case. Whichever route you take, it is important that the contractor has a good knowledge of the Musicians' Union agreements and that the producer has made known his estimated music budget to the composer/contractor from the outset. If these simple precautions are followed then specially composed and recorded music can provide exceptional value for money.

The use of library 'mood' music has great advantages, but its real cost has often been obscured by the budgeting systems of the broadcasting companies. Remember that £4,000 would not be an untypical fee for two minutes of nationally transmitted recorded music and for this you would not get exclusivity. However, specially recorded and composed music will be tailored to the needs of your programme and you may be pleasantly surprised at the value you get.

Obviously a programme whose subject matter suggests small musical resources will work out much cheaper than something that demands a symphonic treatment. The function of film music is to set or enhance the emotional atmosphere of a scene. Evening in a Spanish garden is easily suggested by a few chords on a solo guitar. However, evoking the Charge of the Light Brigade with brass and percussion is going to be more costly.

The most important thing is to have a resourceful composer who knows how much your production can financially bear. The advent of electronic instruments gives a potential range of sound to one or two musicians which would have been impossible some years back without a large band. The producer needs to decide at the outset exactly how much music is needed. Many excellent productions, including dramas, have dispensed with music entirely beyond that used in opening and closing credits. Natural location sound if often the most effective and many redundant music sequences have been included for no better reason than that the location recordist has gone to sleep, or the editor has wanted to use up a lot of pretty shots, or the script has run out of things to say.

The use of wall-to-wall atmospheric music in the Hollywood tradition may be appropriate to an American soap opera but can be obtrusive and irrelevant for a small screen drama or documentary. Directors might keep in mind the term used by film musicians for the habit of underscoring every mood change with musical emphasis; Mickey Mousing.

If you can afford it, you can get a full orchestral sound from only fourteen players so long as they are properly recorded and remixed. Music for television should not require the musicians to over-dub. Don't ask two trumpets to play again on a second pass of a tape thus making four trumpets. However you can ask the woodwind to double so that a clarinettist for example might be required to play a flute or saxophone as they might be asked to do in a live orchestra, just so long as it involves one pass of the tape.

The standard session for incidental music is three hours long to include one break of fifteen minutes. The maximum amount of music it is feasible to tape in this period is twenty four minutes.

This just applies to out of vision recording. If you want your musicians to appear on camera for example to give backing to a singer, they will receive a higher fee and you may need to book two sessions, one for rehearsal and one for the shooting. Remember, both will have to be paid for. Musicians used to mime to their own, or to someone else's music are paid a special rate and in the latter case the permission of the original musicians has to be obtained.

A problem, as in most areas of copyright, is the multiple and growing number of applications of videotape. Your agreement with a musician will not necessarily buy you all rights. In short, once you've done the recording session and paid the bill you may not then sell your programme as a video, put it on pay television, sell it to satellite station, or show it in a cinema without paying an extra fee. There is a scale of charges known as Further Use Fees by which you can buy additional rights to cover outlets not included in a standard agreement, so the wise producer will save a lot of trouble by deciding in advance whether he is going for terrestrial transmission in the UK, European distribution, world rights, sale on tape or disc, or so on.

Although most professional musicians are represented by the Musicians Union (MU) this is not invariably the case. Soloists, and some chamber music ensembles, may be represented by the Incorporated Society of Musicians (ISM). Their members are likely to include both instrumental and vocal soloists, orchestral and ballet conductors, choral conductors and accompanists, and church organists. Military bands are represented by the MU, church choirs come under ISM agreements.

Performing rights

Enforcing copyright of a book is a fairly straightforward matter. The evidence for any serious plagiarism is permanent and in a concrete form. With music the problems are more difficult. Although the pirating of a musical score or lyric is easily tracked down a performance is an ephemeral event, and recorded music dubbed into a television sound track will be in fragmentary form and often combined with dialogue or sound effects. For most of the 19th century it was held that once a tune had been published anybody could sing, play, copy or record it to their heart's content. According to legend, the tables were turned when a bunch of aggrieved composers in Paris went around restaurants with resident orchestras or accordianists and refused to pay for their drinks until the management paid for their music. Dramatic Gallic gestures were one thing but this was not a reliable technique for ensuring that music publishers and composers got paid for their work. After much lobbying the 1911 Copyright Act did give composers in the United Kingdom exclusive rights to the public performance of their works but it made no provision for an effective means of collection. This problem was solved in 1914 by the creation of the Performing Right Society.

Today the Society administers the collection of royalties on behalf of its composer and publisher members. Composers assign to the PRS three of the rights embodied in the 1988 Copyright Act. These are the right publicly to perform a work, the right to broadcast it and the right to include it in a cable programme service. These three rights are known collectively as the performing right.

Note that this right is in addition to the rights to record or dub music which make up the quite separate issue of Mechanical Copyright.

Rather than have hundreds of composers and publishers policing thousands of production companies, concert venues, halls, pubs, clubs and anywhere where music is played, PRS operates a licence system with a scale of tariffs applicable to the different types of premises and use of music. The resulting revenues are then distributed amongst the members of the PRS in the UK and to foreign societies representing composers abroad. Significant music users like broadcasters have to submit very detailed returns of every piece of music used so that an equitable share out can be made amongst the various interested parties. Pubs and shops on the other hand pay a straight annual licence fee.

The public's awareness of its copyright obligations probably hasn't advanced much since the 19th century and enforcement often leads to expressions of outrage. Nonetheless any music used outside a domestic or private circle is subject to PRS licensing, even piped music in aircraft or waiting rooms. The PRS is very active in enforcing its rights. It employs around seven hundred staff and licenses around 200, 000 organizations. Nonetheless the greatest revenues come from radio, television and films, so even if your enterprise is no more than a humble sales video for a travel agent or is intended for a public showing at the Polytechnic Film Club you ought to have declared yourselves and ensured that the venue has a licence. If you or your client is caught improperly using music the PRS can seek a court order to stop all future musical performances and it can sue for damages. If you use or perform music and then belatedly ask for PRS licensing the Society will impose a 50% surcharge on the first year's licence fee. If you are challenged and continue to operate without the payment for an appropriate license you will almost certainly have to appear in court. Even if the damages alone may not be great these can, combined with the costs, total several thousand pounds. The PRS licenses principally the organizations which cause a performance to be played, and in the past this part of the administration has been largely the concern of the broadcast companies. Apart from the irritation of having to fill in returns for music used, individual producers and directors could forget the matter. But with increasing numbers of productions occurring with small companies who are squeezed by rigorously controlled budgets a director has to make allowance for the likely cost implications of music used in his work, and needs to be clear who is going to pick up the bill.

If your field is corporate video your standard contract will probably have a clause stating that you guarantee to provide your final tape clear of all further copyright and licensing obligations. If the client gets caught by the PRS, or any other of the copyright agencies, he will be able to seek redress from you. All types of music have to be accounted for, including that used during the main body of the programme as background as well as that used in opening or closing sequences or in overtly musical items. Even the recordings used to accompany late night test cards have a special rate and have to be declared after being broadcast.

PRS licences for broadcasters are based on a number of considerations such as potential audience size. On a scale of payments all national radio and television channels are calculated at 100% of the national fee and smaller organizations are discounted accordingly. For example, in 1991 the late Thames Television paid 19.4% of the national fee whilst BBC Radio Orkney got away with a mere 0.04%! Commercial local radio stations paid a straight levy of between 5–9% of their advertising revenues. Stations dedicated to talks programmes paid only 2%. It all added up to over £40 million pounds worth of revenue from Great Britain and Ireland, derived from the broadcasting and cable companies alone.

Even so the PRS cannot guarantee to be able to clear all music. One problem can arise from the use of musical film clips in a compilation programme. Musical film items or performances recorded in the USA may involve dramatic rights which are beyond the remit of the PRS. So don't automatically assume that so long as you come clean with the PRS you can help yourself to music from a film sound track. For example the producers of a programme about the life of a musical star might renegotiate an exclusivity for the original numbers or arrangements with surviving copyright holders. Traditional music may not always be free. An ancient folk tune is clearly public property, but it is probably familiar from a known arrangement and the arrangement may well be the copyright of a composer. Copyright in more exotic folk music may exist. The performers on Burundi nose flutes may play non copyright melodies, but the collector who made the original field recording or the musician who transcribed the score subsequently might well claim payment.

Despite all this the individual director should not usually get problems from the implications of performing right. Mechanical rights are a little more hazardous.

Mechanical rights

The PRS only grants permission to perform or broadcast a work. It does not have anything to do with the authorization of others to record a work or to copy or dub work from existing recordings. These are known as the mechanical rights and are policed quite separately by the Mechanical Copyright Protection Society.

The MCPS represents thousands of music composers and publishers and acts for them as their agent. It has ties with similar overseas organizations and, in the United Kingdom, represents over a million overseas members. The Society negotiates fees with those who want to record or dub music and collects and distributes royalties deriving from the recording whether in the form of discs and tapes for sale or used in audio visual or broadcast media. Mechanical royalties are not only due when a director incorporates a section of a commercial disc in his programme. Even if a character in a drama warbles a few lines of a ditty which is in copyright, the permission of the copyright owner is due and this will come under mechanical rights.

There may be more than one right involved. With a commercial recording there will be a copyright owner of the recording itself, for example a pop group, but there is a different right in the tunes or lyrics which they use assuming that these are not totally original or unquestionably traditional. Both copyright owners will have to be contacted by MCPS before the music can be cleared for use in a production. If this were not enough there is a third copyright involved in all commercial recordings which is that of the record company itself and their permission has to be asked independently of the MCPS procedures.

The forerunner of the MCPS was set up in 1910 during the run-up to the 1911 Copyright Act. The curious name reflects the fact that at the time the best known way of recording a composer's work was by using rolls of punched paper tape in mechanical pianos, or by various systems of hand cranked drums and punch cards in street barrel organs. But from the time of its inception the organization had its sights on the emerging gramophone companies. For a long time revenue derived from a duty stamp affixed to the covers of gramophone records, and today the MCPS logo is incorporated in the design of recording sleeves and labels. Today the MCPS takes 8.5% of the published dealer's price for compact discs, cassettes etc.

Despite the technological changes which have brought us digital recording and laser discs the term mechanical rights has stuck and is enshrined in law. Under the 1988 Act the rights of composers are in line with those of other authors and continue for fifty years from death. An exception is the copyright in the recording itself which lasts for fifty years from the first publication.

Mechanical rights can give the director real headaches. Whereas performing right is normally the responsibility of the transmitting company, or can be dispensed with through obtaining the relevant licence by smaller organizations, the clearance of mechanical rights is neither certain nor simple and lands squarely in the lap of the producer or director. The most important point is that permission to use a work has to be obtained in advance. Whether you are a record producer using copyright compositions or arrangements, a director dubbing a sound-track, or a documentary maker incorporating commercial music into his story you must clear the rights *first*. Failure to do this can result in an injunction to prevent the showing of the work or a claim for damages. Moreover, not all clearances are quick and automatic. Not all recording companies are represented by MCPS; overseas labels are a particular headache. If your production involves worldwide distribution, or is intended for multiple use, such as both transmitted television and subsequent sale on video cassette, you can get into lengthy negotiations. Indeed problems with recordings and record companies are one of the reasons for the revival of specially composed and recorded music.

If you refer your chosen music to the MCPS licensing department too late, and it cannot be cleared, you may be landed with some very inconvenient and expensive last minute changes. If in doubt always have a second choice or an alternative version up your sleeve. Murphy will ensure that the one recording you have set your sights on is the one which is not clearable.

The opening of the national broadcast channels to independents has raised a few questions. In the past MCPS has simplified matters by establishing blanket agreements with the BBC, ITV and the main satellite companies. This, together with the existence of full time copyright clearance departments, took away most of the bother from individuals so long as they took early advice on whether or not music could be cleared. The current state of play is that independents working for transmission are regarded as sub-contractors to the transmitting organization, and so have limited rights to use the music of MCPS members in certain productions. The advice is to approach the MCPS yourself to see if your clearances can come under any blanket agreement, and check with the commissioning organization who will pick up any bill. Royalties are supposed to be paid up front and licences are issued within twenty-one days of the receipt of the fees agreed. Although the MCPS, and relevant specialists in a broadcasting service, will have an idea of normal costs all fees are negotiable and the director on a tight budget may be taken aback by some of the royalties demanded. Prices are variable. Permission may be refused outright if you intend to use the music for parody, or have your own modification or new arrangement in mind. You will be asked to tell MCPS the uses to which the music will be put and may be asked to submit a script or relevant résumé. In some cases the production and copyright holders may be brought together for direct negotiations, although usually the Society will try to act as negotiator and honest broker and administer the invoicing and collection of royalties.

The more details you can give the MCPS about titles, publishers, record companies, duration of extract and details of the programme the better. You will, however, be expected to repeat such information later on a music cue sheet to be submitted to the MCPS.

The MCPS will also advise you how to set about tracing copyright holders of non MCPS recordings. Non broadcast audio visual productions are as subject to MCPS licensing as their big brothers in broadcasting. This includes corporate and training videos, audio-visual slide presentations, closed circuit and even student projects. Prior clearance is essential. Naturally though, a fee for an in-house training video will attract lower royalty charges than a feature film for international distribution. An increasing amount of television production now depends on complex co-production deals, sponsorship rights and secondary sales in videogramme form. The result is that copyright can become fragmented with different distributors or companies negotiating different rights in different countries and under different copyright laws. Deals involving music rights in both the EEC and the USA can be particularly problematical when it comes to using commercial recordings. A whole set of clearances may be involved with the constant risk that the failure of one might put in jeopardy all the rest. You can only try to limit the risk where you select only British recordings by MCPS members, where you intend to use the music for a single purpose in a single country, and when you have ascertained that there is a fair fee which your budget will bear.

Alas this simple state of affairs is less and less common. The increasingly complex international world of video publishing, satellite transmission, cable and the spread of the camcorder will be matched by increasing complexity in achieving copyright clearances and increasing difficulties is collecting royalties due. The outcome is a matter for conjecture but it should be possible to predict an increasing toughness by the copyright protection societies, increasing evasion by design or ignorance, and a desire for companies and authors to contract enhanced 'all rights' single payment deals on the basis that reliance upon royalties or residuals will be increasingly a problem.

Production music

Production music (mood music as it is commonly called) looks like a perfect solution to the problems and difficulties of mechanical copyright clearances and the specialized interest involved in commissioning and recording your own score. There are around fifty specialist music publishers in the UK alone, and considerably more catalogues available, which provide speciallv composed and recorded music tracks for film, video and audio visual presentation uses. They have enormous advantages. First there are many thousands of tracks available ranging from drum taps at different tempi, rhythms and durations up to full orchestral recordings of popular classics. There are collections of every sort of ethnic folk music and specially composed collections of short stings for programme junctions and commercial breaks.

The only obvious disadvantage is that production music is not exclusive, unless someone buys exclusivity for a signature tune, and some of the better tracks do crop up regularly in different contexts. The recurrence of pieces from such an enormous number of tracks does give the game away. A great deal of this music is lacking in any kind of musical merit. The uncritical use of wall-to-wall musical drivel is the hallmark of poor corporate videos. On the other hand most libraries are re-issuing their collections as high quality compact discs and many distinguished musicians have put their compositions, arrangements or performances onto mood music disc, sometimes under their own names.

Many of the best known signature tunes and themes from radio and television programmes were found on production music recordings. Most recordings are performed anonymously by groups of session musicians or else pseudonymously or by whimsically named groups like the Rutland Philharmonia or Alfonso's Hot Tamales. In reality these might well be part of an internationally reputed orchestra or a much respected jazz band. Some libraries provide parts of their collections free, or for a small charge, to established broadcasting companies, dubbing theatres and large facility houses. Smaller production companies can also build up good collection, which may include sound effects, for a modest cost.

The lone operator can approach selected companies direct and seek advice which may be provided free or for a small fee depending on whether the music research can be done personally. The choice of music is so critical to a programme that it is worthwhile spending as much time as you can afford selecting the right tracks. If you do not think so, or have a liking for piped music in hotels and airports, just accept that you have tin ears and no musical judgement and get someone else to choose the music for you, preferably the film or videotape editor.

Of course any single library you approach will only suggest its own recordings.

Apart from the obvious convenience of production music there are clinching financial reasons for turning to it. The production companies are represented by the MCPS and all such music is effectively cleared for copyright so there is no pre-recording or transmission formality to perform. Although there are no clearance formalities you are expected to purchase a licence from MCPS and sign a code of conduct committing yourself to declaring all music used on a cue sheet provided, to give details of any international implications, and to pay up in advance of transmission or public showing. Because of the ease of access to mood music discs, the lack of administrative niggles, and their apparent abundance in cutting rooms, dubbing theatres, libraries and production offices, there are many in television production who regard them as almost free. Fees often have been swallowed up in the various blanket agreements of broadcast companies.

Under innovative accounting systems in the broadcast companies and the financial squeeze on those operating in the independent sector, it is being driven home that library music is anything but free. Even in videos solely for closed circuit use the cost begins at £15 per thirty seconds for United Kingdom usage alone, which can be a fair proportion of the budget in a twenty minute corporate presentation with music throughout. If the video is for sale the cost is £30 for world rights for one hundred copies rising to £100 per thirty seconds for European rights, and £100 for world rights. Ordinary single UK television programmes attract a modest £33 per half minute but all rights, including retail sales or rental, can cost £250.

Music in advertisements attracts higher scales. World rights can cost up to £2200 per minute transmitted. Commercials may not be long but they get shown an awful lot of times. There is a detailed schedule of payments issued by the MCPS. Fees are the same regardless of which publisher supplies the recording. You may not be out of the woods yet. The PRS protects the copyright of composers and their publishers in the performance and broadcast of their work. The MCPS protects all copyright holders against the unauthorized dubbing or recording of their work. These don't cover a third right which is the right of record companies over the broadcasting or playing in public of an existing recording. The record companies collect their dues via another organization, Phonographic Performance Ltd.

Everywhere that commercial recordings are played from the BBC to the owner of a juke box needs to purchase a licence from PPL as well as PRS. PPL spends a considerable amount of effort in litigation to establish its rights and its revenues come to several million pounds a year. About two thirds of this revenue is distributed amongst the record companies but the rest is used to bridge the one significant gap in music copyright. Musicians lack legal protection so PPL operates a series of *ex gratia* payments on their behalf. A proportion of the remaining income of PPL is distributed to named performers and groups credited on the labels of PPL, affiliated companies. What is left is given as a lump sum to the Musicians Union for the general benefit of its members. There is no way in which the unseen and uncredited army of session performers could be individually identified and rewarded.

The rights of record companies vary greatly from country to country and some governments refuse to accept the right of recording companies to withhold permission for the use of published recordings, although the right to a reasonable remuneration afterwards is established. PPL is not a major headache for the broadcast sector director. As with the PRS, blanket agreements exist. But you should be aware that if you decide to dub a commercial track and have clearances from MCPS and PRS these permissions are contingent upon the possession of an appropriate PPL license before the final work may be published or broadcast in any way.

But there can be hitches. PPL does not clear foreign labels. For the use of foreign recordings, including American ones, reference has to be made to the International Federation of the Phonographic Industry (IFPI). The IFPI may give broadcast rights to a production for UK or EEC purposes only but if you need world rights or have co-production in mind the clearances may become complex and expensive. Finally the right to dub existing commercial record labels is held by British Phonographic Industry Ltd (BPI). BPI has blanket agreements with the main broadcasters and represents most of the British companies. Again its agreement only covers the use of British labels in a UK context. If world rights are on the cards individual companies may still refuse permission.

It should by now be clear why in the non-broadcast sector directors tend to flee from the idea of using commercial recordings at all and limit themselves normally to safe old programme music recordings, or commission original work.

There is one remaining area of complexity. Some works are classed as dramatico-musical productions. This is the term used to describe operas, stage musicals and ballet. If you intend to include any such material in your production you have to get every clearance in advance. There are special problem areas to look out for. A libretto has a copyright separate from that from the rights in the music. One may be copyright but not the other. If the libretto is an English translation of a foreign original and is of modern provenance then it will be copyrighted. The choreography of a ballet or musical may be copyrighted and so may subtitles. A musical score may be ancient but if it appears in a newly edited edition it may also be subject to rights. Note that this applies to recordings of works other than feature films. That is a completely new can of worms.

CHAPTER 8

Blasphemy, race, sedition and sex

In less tolerant ages the boundary between what society considered a sin and what it considered a crime was very different from today. Nonetheless there remain a number of laws on the statute book reflecting traditional moral attitudes. Sometimes laws which are generally thought to have been repealed are re-discovered alive and kicking. Enlightened people probably regard the laws on blasphemy to be as relevant to modern thought as the witchcraft laws of the 16th century. But not everyone holds this opinion. A poll of BBC heads of production departments in the 1980s showed that they received more public complaints about blasphemy on the screen than they did about either sex or violence. The public were often deeply offended by the use of commonplace oaths like 'God!' or 'Jesus!' and even by terms which had for centuries lost their religious connotations like 'Bloody' which seemed to be able to upset even those who had no idea that it was a corruption of 'By Our Lady!'

Blasphemy in law is strictly defined and is precisely limited to libels upon the tenets of the Church of England. It occurs when there is an indecent description of sacred objects or outrageous comments on God, holy personages or articles of the Anglican faith. It is the violence of the expression of anti-Christian views which is the touchstone, and only if those expressed views are deemed likely to lead to a breach of the peace will the law be invoked. So attacks upon the Anglican religion are acceptable so long as inflammatory or scurrilous language is not used.

In 1923 a successful prosecution was brought against a persistent soap box orator and pamphleteer who repeatedly outraged the religious sensibilities of passengers at Stratford East railway station. Thereafter the law lay dormant. Either nobody said anything outrageous enough to provoke the risk of a horse-whipping, or more secular generations lost the ability to be outraged. In 1977 the law sprung back to life. Mrs Mary Whitehouse, leader of the National Viewers' and Listeners' Organization, brought a private prosecution against the magazine *Gay News*. In it a poem had appeared describing the feelings towards Christ of a homosexual Roman centurion and implying that Jesus had performed homosexual acts. *Gay News* was fined £1,000 and its editor £500 with a suspended prison sentence, put aside on appeal, of nine months.

Far from unleashing a spate of similar prosecutions this led to a re-examination of the blasphemy laws. It was widely held that a law which protected exclusively the Anglican church, and no other sect or religion, was quite irrelevant to a plural society. On one hand there were calls for the law to be repealed, on the other for it to be replaced by a more general one extending protection from gross offence to all other religions. Since the forcibly expressed tenets of almost any one religion can be considered grossly offensive to another, the problems of legal definition killed any idea of new legislation.

In 1990 the issue exploded over the publication of the book *The Satanic Verses* by Salman Rushdie and a subsequent death sentence passed upon the author by the Iranian religious leader Ayatollah Khomeini. What was taken to be an insult to the Prophet Mohammed did indeed lead to public outrage and violence. British Muslims tried to invoke the law on blasphemy but as the existing law applied only to the Church of England the Queen's Bench Divisional Court refused to allow the prosecution to proceed. Opponents of Rushdie subsequently tried two alternative tacks. Seditious libel is one of those offences that slumbers in the statute book but can be dragged into the daylight in extreme circumstances.

Seditious libel is very precisely defined. To be seditious a libel must bring into contempt the Royal family, the Government and Constitution, the Houses of Parliament, or the administration of the law. Moreover such a libel must incite the British public to use unlawful means to overthrow the institutions of the state, raise discontent or promote hostility between different classes. So an attack upon the Royal family might be offensive to monarchists but would not in itself constitute a seditious libel, but an incitement to set up the guillotine in Trafalgar Square clearly would. The British Muslims tried to prosecute Salman Rushdie for sedition on the grounds that he had created hostility between British classes and damaged the relations of the British Government with Muslim foreign states.

The prosecution was thrown out on the grounds that *The Satanic Verses* did not meet the requirement that it incited violence against the lawful authority of the state. Moreover not only should such a work have incited violence but actual violence or defiance of the law should have resulted for a prosecution to have succeeded. It is noteworthy that seditious libel is not regularly invoked against Irish Republican groups who overtly call for the violent overthrow of the institutions of the state, although as discussed below, the special circumstances of Northern Ireland have led to restrictions of great importance to television programme makers.

The third legal assault upon Salman Rushdie was through a new piece of legislation, The Public Order Act 1987. Under that Act it is an offence to display, publish or distribute material which is threatening, abusive or insulting and 'intends to stir up racial hatred or if racial hatred may be stirred up thereby under the circumstances.' So as with the offence of blasphemy it is not enough to have expressed racist views but the language used should have been violent and inflammatory. Racial hatred is defined as 'hatred against a group of persons in Great Britain defined by reference to colour, race, nationality (including citizenship) or ethnic or national origins'. Religion was specifically excluded and the question arose as to how this would apply to racial groups defined also by a common religion. Could for an example a violent attack upon the tenets of Judaism constitute a racial attack upon Jews? The proviso 'under the circumstances' is also important in that a strongly worded reported speech or published correspondence might be merely offensive under some circumstances but might be actionable at others, for example at a time of actual racial unrest and public disorder. Prosecutions may only be brought by the Attorney General. The Muslim attack upon Rushdie failed because it could not be accepted that Muslims constituted a defined racial group, nor could the book merely by being offensive to their beliefs constitute an incitement to violence or hatred against them. It was widely asked at the time rather why the Public Order Act was not invoked against those publicly demanding the assassination of a British subject.

It seems therefore that the laws governing sedition, race and blasphemy are so rarely invoked, and the circumstances necessary to be so extreme that actual prosecution is unlikely.

However the broadcaster is in a far weaker position than the newspaper editor whose only restraint, apart from the law, is the comparatively weak Press Council. When the independent television companies were set up in 1954 they were required by the Television Act 1954 to observe high standards of taste and decency. Whatever this really meant it clearly implied a more stringent control than the letter of the law. In the same way the BBC is committed 'that so far as possible the programmes for which they are responsible should not offend against good taste or decency . . . or be offensive to public feeling'. Definitions are slippery. The BBC issues guidelines to producers which outline the problem without getting us much further towards a solution.

> The borderline between taste and decency is narrow. One useful distinction is to regard decency as a fundamental value while taste is a matter of manners. What is acceptable at one time and in one set of circumstances may not be in another.

There has grown up a veritable neurosis amongst broadcasters dedicated to ensuring that programmes should avoid giving offence to ethnic minorities, religious minorities, sexual groups, the old, the disabled and women in general. Some directors have come to think that it is dangerous to portray a comic character with a stutter. The use of terms like black, elderly, crippled, handicapped, or even chairman or spokesman are subjects of debate and concern. There is no doubt that television programme makers are advised to be ahead of the letter of the law in responding to changing public attitudes. Despite the rearguard action of campaigners like Mrs Whitehouse, the graphic portrayal of sexual acts has become frequent and full nudity not uncommon on the cinema and television screens. It may be that the director has less to fear from public reaction by portraying sexual intercourse than by condoning sexual stereotypes.

The frank treatment of sexual matters on television seems to concern the titillating tabloid press more than the bulk of the viewing population and certainly seems to cause less concern than issues of cruelty and violence or even bad language. Television and radio transmissions are specifically excluded from the Obscene Publications Act 1959 but films, and latterly videotapes, are not. The old test of obscenity is that:

> *The tendency of the matter charged as obscene is to deprave and corrupt those whose minds are open to such immoral influences and into whose hands a publication of this sort may fall.*

Generally the law has made an ass of itself whenever it has tried to define what tends to corrupt and who precisely is supposed to tend to be corrupted. The Act also stipulates that the tendency to deprave and corrupt must exist in relation to all relevant circumstances causing people 'to read see or hear' the offending article. In other words the court has to take account of the nature of the readership or audience. The successful prosecution of the magazine *Oz* in 1974 was upheld because of a scurrilous edition compiled by and specifically distributed to schoolboys. The case provided one of the most entertaining trials of the decade.

Although overtly pornographic television programmes are not being shown at present on British television, such programmes are regularly broadcast on the continent of Europe and can be picked up from satellite by those with the curiosity and technical ability. Whether or not it is an offence to record or subsequently privately disseminate tapes of such programmes under the Obscene Publications Act is not certain. It certainly would breach copyright if done without proper clearances. Tapes or films accused of obscenity may be impounded by the police who may seek a warrant to enter premises and confiscate obscene articles, and HM Customs and Excise may impound obscene materials at a port of entry. It is illegal to send obscene matter through the post. The Act provides specifically for films and offers the defence that they may be 'justified as being for the public good on the ground that it is in the interests of drama, opera, ballet or any other art or literature or learning.' The onus of proof rests with the defendant.

If a case does come to court a jury must decide whether obscenity exists or not, which will depend on their own attitudes or prejudices. If you are involved in erotic productions the vague but generally accepted line seems to be between soft and hard pornography, with the latter definitely falling foul of the law if it portrays acts which are in themselves clearly illegal such as sexual acts involving minors or animals. However, hard pornography, depicting explicit genital contact between adults is permissable in practically all European countries, the United Kingdom and Ireland being notable exceptions. Under EEC directives there must be free transmission of information across national frontiers. The clash between the Home Office and the satellite station *Red Hot Dutch* is the first battle in what promises to be a long and potentially very entertaining struggle.

It is highly unlikely so far that any British television director in the broadcast sector would be allowed to show anything running a risk of prosecution.

Complaints procedures

If a viewer wishes to complain about a programme he may choose to approach one of the three statutory regulatory bodies.

The first of these is the *Broadcasting Complaints Commission* (BCC) set up by the Broadcasting Act 1981. Its brief is to adjudicate upon complaints of unjust or unfair treatment in programmes and unwarranted infringement of privacy in programmes and in connection with their preparation. Most significantly it does not adjudicate on matters of taste. It may only adjudicate upon programmes which have actually been broadcast and not upon the general conduct of companies or of broadcasters. Moreover it will only hear complaints from those who have a direct interest in the programmes in question or who have participated in them. General public complaints are not within its jurisdiction.

If the BCC takes up a grievance it will demand a written reply from the company concerned and may demand to see the programme. If it finds against the programme its only sanction to demand that its findings be published prominently either in print or on air.

The BCC was described as a 'pain in the neck' by Alasdair Milne, then Managing Director of BBC Television. The reaction was shared by many broadcasters at the time on the grounds that the Governors of the BBC and the Independent Broadcasting Authority (IBA) had perfectly good procedures and guidelines of their own. The uproar paled to insignificance compared to that which resulted from the setting up of the *Broadcasting Standards Council* (BSC) under the 1990 Broadcasting Act. The remit of the BSC is specifically to watch over the portrayal of violence, sex and matters of taste and decency. There were accusations of censorship and a new Inquisition fuelled by a feeling that the Government was in a mood of wild paranoia about television and was determined to curb its perceived excesses. In fact it seems that the programme maker does have little to fear from the Council. If a viewer or listener wishes to complain the Council may ask for a viewing copy or sound tape of the programme concerned and may or may not hold a hearing in which both the complainant and the broadcaster may be asked to attend. If the Council finds against the broadcasters it may demand that such findings be published in the press or on air at the expense of the company concerned. A regular summary of complaints and findings will be published by the Council. The Council's remit covers all broadcasts, including cable and satellite, but specifically excludes matters of accuracy or bias in topical or political programmes. It has produced its own code of practice to add to the guidelines and codes of practice which everybody else seems to have produced of late. As its area of activity is limited and its sanctions negligible it may simply turn out as a harmless quango and talking shop for the small interest groups which are determined to find in television the source of all evil. The BSC is the body empowered to investigate complaints about commercials.

The body which has the greatest capacity for regulation is the *Independent Television Commission* (ITC) which since 1991 has had the job of licensing and regulating all television services in the United Kingdom whether terrestrial, cable, satellite, teletext or locally distributed via microwave. Only distribution systems capable of reaching fewer than a thousand homes, or confined to a single building such as a block of flats, are exempt from ITC jurisdiction. The Commission has replaced the Independent Broadcasting Authority and the Cable Authority but is confined to television matters since radio broadcasters now have their own *Radio Authority*.

A lot of the work of ITC is concerned with the setting of technical standards, the regulation of new services and means of distribution. For the programme maker its most important products are its Code of Advertising Standards and Practice, and its Programme Code.

The former is based broadly on the principles laid down by the advertising industry's own Broadcasting Standards Council beginning with the exhortation that all advertisements should be legal, decent, honest and truthful. It then gives detailed guidance covering eventualities from the portrayal of animals, use of newsreaders, alcoholic drinks, patent medicines, religious advertising and so on. There is an additional code concerning programme sponsorship.

The Programme Code contains both specific rules binding on all licencee companies and more general guidelines similar to those issued by the BBC to its producers.

The ITC does have teeth. Complaints from the public are investigated and errors of judgement can be punished. A company may be told to drop a programme, make cuts, or broadcast an apology. A company may be fined or have the period of its licence curtailed. The ultimate sanction would be the withdrawal of the licence to broadcast. In the case of advertisements the output is monitored locally and any offending commercials may be withdrawn or amended with immediate effect, again with severe penalties for companies failing to comply.

How rigidly the ITC will be able to maintain a consistency of control remains to be seen. Its remit cover an exploding number of channels and means of delivery, including teletext services, and the broadcasters are having to fight for ever smaller slices of the revenue cake in consequence. For example neither advertisers nor sponsors are allowed any editorial influence over programme content, and the recent habit of 'product placement' is strictly forbidden. Denouncing such occurrences and detecting or preventing them may be two very different things, particularly when the broadcast companies are themselves becoming publishers of the works of smaller production houses. Will the producer of a travel programme with an inadequate budget tell the truth about the tour operator who sponsored the tickets? Are some children's cartoons any more than commercials for spin-off merchandise from T-shirts to video games, particularly when these are also advertised on television? Has cash changed hands so that an actor or comedian drinks from a can of one brand of Cola and not another, and has the programme content been in any way modified to ensure that the audience takes good notice? Old hands can recall BBC days when it was a dismissable offence for accepting favours to plug a book or record, when tailplanes and airline logos were cut from films, and designers had to block out trademarks from cereal packets or fabricate fictitious sauce bottle labels.

Financial pressures on broadcasters from sponsors and the advertisers may well turn out to present the programme makers with their biggest headaches in the coming decade rather than any official attempts to regulate their work.

Any television commercial transmitted on national networks comes under the remit of the ITC. There is an increasing use of film and video for advertising and promotional material for videocassette distribution, closed circuit or other 'videogramme' use. Such overt sponsorship and advertising underpins the whole corporate video sector of the industry. However, working within this area will not completely free you from supervision.

Since the harmonization of the laws of the EEC and the United Kingdom under the Control of Misleading Advertisement Regulations 1988 these matters are subject to the regulation of the Director General of the Office of Fair Trading. You cannot be prosecuted for issuing a misleading advertisement but you can be obliged to cease publication if complaints are upheld. An advertisement is misleading if it contains demonstrably false statements, if it conceals or omits important facts or if it makes promises to do something it has no intention of carrying out. In blatant cases the Director General may apply to the courts for an injunction to curtail publication until an investigation into the validity of charges. Failure to comply would be Contempt of Court.

In practice the Director General has delegated his authority to hear and settle complaints from the public to the *Advertising Standards Authority* (ASA). The ASA was set up in 1961 by the advertising industry and, like the Board of Film Classification and the Press Council, is one of those curiously English self-regulatory bodies which has no legal authority yet has acquired quasi official status. In its own words 'The system is not simply one of self discipline and does not depend upon the individual conscience as its only sanction. Self-regulation goes beyond the regulation of the individual by himself and connotes the regulation of a whole profession by its practitioners acting together.' What this boils down to is that the ASA draws up a Code of Advertising Practice covering all British advertising, with the specific exception of that coming within the remit of the Independent Television Commission. As with the other codes of practice discussed here, it combines generally stated objectives and standards with actual rules against which complaints may be heard and judgements given.

The Code singles out particular areas of difficulty such as advertising claims in relation to health, cosmetic and slimming products, and mail order, financial and business opportunity advertising. Tobacco advertising is strictly controlled, largely as a response to political pressures from outside the advertising industry. Advertising and the portrayal of alcoholic drinks are also currently under pressure.

Like the Press Council, on which it models itself, the ASA has almost no power to impose its will. It may request an advertisement to be withdrawn pending an enquiry and any advertiser judged to have broken the Code may be asked to make a public undertaking to make the alterations demanded and not to repeat the offence. If an offender then thumbs its nose at the Authority all it can do is to ask all other members of the ASA to refuse to handle the campaign in question. A recent example has been a controversy over the use of news photographs of famine, war and disease to draw attention to a brand of sports clothing. The ASA threatened to withdraw access to poster hoardings. How the ASA would or could invoke disciplinary sanctions against indecent, dishonest or misleading video presentations is hard to guess.

British Board of Film Classification

Those involved in making films, including commercials, for theatrical showing or videos for public sale or hire will have to pay attention to the independent body called the British Board of Film Classification (BBFC) still commonly but wrongly called by its original name, Board of Film Censors.

The Board was formed in 1912 by the film industry to get around the problem of having every film to be distributed passed for approval by the watch committee of every local authority in turn. It was set up to prove that the cinema could regulate itself and give a guarantee to local authorities about the wholesomeness of products which had received a certificate.

Over the years the nature of classification has changed from a dual U (Under Fourteen) and A (Adult) categories through various permutations to the current categories:

- 'U' (Universal) i.e. suitable for children of any age

- 'PG' (Parental Guidance) which implies possible mild violence or frightening material though no overt sexual activity.

- '12' a new category introduced in 1989 recognizes that early teenagers are likely to be more sexually aware and sophisticated than their counterparts of previous generations and could take stronger fare.

- '15' rated films include impressionistic sexual acts and the portrayal of some violence and bad language
- '18' assumes adulthood and maturity and replaces the old 'X' category.
- 'R18' category films show graphic sexual acts and may be distributed only through licensed outlets such as sex shops and club cinemas. Ironically, these are often as explicit as those being transmitted publically in the EEC which have caused such a furore in Britain when published by satellite.

Contrary to popular opinion the Board has no legal status with regard to film censorship and it remains a voluntary body. The licensing authorities for cinemas are still the local government authorities and they remain the final arbiters. In practice most of them treat the Board's classification as having legal status and once a classification has been given it normally becomes illegal for a cinema manager to admit minors to showings which the Board has deemed unsuitable. Pity the poor cinema managers trying to work out which adolescents are 12, 15 or 18!

If a film has been refused a classification or the distributors refuse to accept the suggested cuts needed to obtain a classification the producers may still apply to individual local authorities for a licence which might well be granted. Some films, often those which become cult movies, were originally refused a classification but were submitted direct to individual authorities and viewed by solemn faced councillors before their initial showing. At a time when the portrayal of sexual acts or nudity was the main point of dispute it was often possible to see films in London and some other cities which were banned elsewhere.

The reverse may also apply. An example is the film *Monty Python's Life of Brian* which was given a 'PG' rating by the BBFC but offended many local councillors of strong religious convictions who regarded the satire as blasphemous, and both the film and videotape were subject to local bans.

Normally it is in the interest of the distributors to seek the widest possible audience unless notoriety is likely to provide the best publicity. The Board can insist on cuts before issuing a certificate and may attend cutting room sessions. Curiously, since it is reckoned that the impact of a production on a paying cinema audience may be different from that upon viewers at home, cuts which were made for theatrical distribution may be restored for the domestic video. All cuts are noted and films may be reclassified or cuts restored in the fullness of time. The *cause célèbre* of today is the fashionable cult or harmless bore of tomorrow.

In 1985 the Video Recordings Act gave the Board a specific legal status by designating it the authority responsible for categorizing all videotapes available for sale, rent or loan. To reflect the spread of video hire a new category 'UC' was introduced to specify material made specifically for small children. With videos the decision of the Board is legally binding although aggrieved producers may appeal to an independent Video Appeals Committee.

Such is the sheer volume of videos produced annually that the Board would sink without trace if it were to try to view every tape, therefore the Act accepts specific exceptions for tapes on sport, religion, music, information or education. In other words the average corporate or instructional video need not be submitted for classification, although if there is to be commercial distribution via retail outlets such a classification might be required as an insurance by the retailers. But if a tape includes sex, violence or genital nudity the exemption no longer applies. Many pop music promotional tapes fall into this category.

As public attitudes have changed so has the status of the Board and there is today less of an emphasis on imposing cuts or preventing distribution than ensuring proper classification. With the granting of 'R18' categories almost any sexual content which does not infringe the Obscene Publications Act will be accepted. 'Video nasties' portraying gross perversions, sadism or cannibalism are unlikely to be submitted in any case. Interestingly the main problems, as defined by the Board itself, are the portrayal of violence, including sexual violence, torture, and the glamorization of drug taking or use of offensive weapons, and the detailed portrayal of how to commit criminal acts or make explosive devices. The sort of bedroom scene which would have had earlier censors screaming for the scissors may today get a very mild classification, whereas an instructional video which in effect shows you how to steal cars would raise greater problems.

Nobody is quite sure how the full accession to the EEC in 1993 will alter things. At present the cable and satellite company BSkyB has voluntarily requested the Board to classify films on its subscription channels and the standards applied are those laid down by the ITC.

CHAPTER 9

Defamation, contempt and other legal problems

The Keystone Cops, pre-1914, Mack Sennett. Still provided by the British Film Institute.

Defamation has always been the bugbear of the newspaper journalist and the broadcaster. From the middle 1980s onwards it has become a nightmare.

Defamation

Defamation comes in two categories, slander and libel.

Slander is verbal defamation and is likely to concern a broadcaster only if, for example, a researcher carelessly makes verbal allegations about one party to another in the course of an investigation.

Libel concerns anything defamatory which is published. Remarks made or reported on radio or television or included in the script of a play are considered to have been published in permanent form and therefore count as libel. This can include an impromptu quip as Jimmy Greaves and London Weekend Television discovered at the 1985 FA cup final where a comment on the referee was held to be libellous.

A statement is libellous if it can be proved to have exposed the plaintiff to hatred, ridicule or contempt; if it has caused him to be shunned or avoided; if it lowers him in the esteem of right thinking members of society; or if it disparages him in his office, profession or trade.

To prove libel the plaintiff has to prove that the statement was actually defamatory, that it could be reasonably understood to refer to him personally and that it had been published to a third party. In essence a libel consists of words which have a damaging effect upon the reputation of the plaintiff. If a statement is damaging, but the reputation of the plaintiff is not hurt then a libel action will not succeed.

It is because the idea of reputation is so bound up with wounded pride and that concepts like 'right thinking members of society' are so vague as to be almost meaningless, that libel actions have been likened to games of poker rather than processes of justice. Libel cases are heard before a jury and the jury is empowered to award damages. The plaintiff does not have to prove that a statement intended to libel. If a statement is defamatory the courts will assume intent. The plaintiff does not have to produce proof that his reputation has suffered harm, simply that a statement 'tends' to damage it. At the end of the day, and libel cases frequently stretch over several years, a great deal depends upon the whim of a jury. There has been a series of judgements which suggest that some juries become seriously unhinged by their untrammelled power to assess the amount of damages.

Newspapers, perhaps sometimes their own worst enemies, have borne the main brunt. In 1987 the current trend to award extortionate levels of damages began with the award to a Navy intelligence agent of £450 000 for remarks made four years previously in a Greek language newspaper with a UK circulation of around fifty. A few months later the politician Jeffrey Archer was awarded £500 000 against *The Star*. In 1989 the *Mail on Sunday* had damages of £470 000 awarded against it for libelling a food firm. In 1988 a small circulation trade magazine *Stationery Trade News* suffered an award of £300 000 for implying the use of counterfeit brand names and in 1990 Sonia Sutcliffe, wife of the 'Yorkshire Ripper' was awarded £600 000 against *Private Eye*.

Since 1990 it has been possible to appeal for a reduction of unreasonable amounts of damages, whereas previously an appeal could only be on the basis of a re-trial. But recent jury awards such as £200 000 against the *Face* magazine in 1992 demonstrate that the trend to award unrealistic levels of damages has not ceased.

Television Companies have not escaped. The threat comes not merely from the extraordinary amounts of damages which juries may award but the certainty of enormous legal costs in fighting a case. For example in 1985 Esther Rantzen and the BBC were sued by a doctor for allegations of professional misconduct. The BBC fought the case for 87 days and finally backed down and settled for £75 000 damages. In the meantime its bill for legal expenses had risen to over one million pounds.

For reasons of cost the libel laws are therefore under severe attack. Awards of hundreds of thousands of pounds to aggrieved but frequently notoriously wealthy and publicity seeking celebrities look indecent compared to the modest awards given to normal citizens who may have suffered permanent mutilation through assault, accident or professional malpractice. Recourse to the courts for defamation is really only a practical option for the wealthy or those who can get wealthy backers. There is no Legal Aid available in civil defamation cases. The wealthy can use the threat of libel to bully and silence critics. Robert Maxwell, the newspaper owner and company speculator, notoriously used the threat of litigation to prevent revelations about his activities although within days of his death it was universally published that he had been known to be one of the greatest swindlers of the century.

The result is that broadcasting organizations, which unlike newspapers cannot even hope to boost circulation figures as a by-product of a juicy libel action, tend to play safe. How many programmes are suppressed or grossly diluted for fear of actions for libel will never be known. Certainly the first instinct of company lawyers faced by the threat of an action will be to attempt an out-of-court settlement.

The only absolute defence in a libel action is that the words are true in substance and in fact. This means that the statement must be factually flawless and free from extraneous innuendo and you must have supporting proof substantiating your statement.

This can involve finding both sure documentary evidence and reliable witnesses. Witnesses may be very unwilling to come forward. Many people will offer help to a television programme only so long as they do not appear in vision. As two or more years may elapse before a case is brought to court memories may have become unreliable or opinions changed. You cannot quote hearsay or rumour, however widespread or clearly well founded, something which the late Robert Maxwell knew and manipulated so well. So a reporter or researcher has to keep extremely clear and factual notebooks and be careful to establish, wherever possible, that his or her witness will be willing to stick by their words in the event of a threat of litigation.

The statement, as said above, must not contain innuendo or extraneous allegations. It may be possible to get away with describing a crooked businessman as a liar and a swindler and justify your defamation, but if in addition you call him a drunk on no more than hearsay evidence you will still have committed an actionable libel. Beware misquoting the plaintiff's own words. For example he may have published his own comments about youthful experiments with narcotics but to allude to him as an addict or drug abuser will leave you open to a libel suit. The 1992 award of £200 000 against the *Face* magazine to a pop star Jason Donovan revolved upon the Plaintiff's published words boasting of his sexual promiscuity. The magazine interpreted the words as including homosexual activities which the pop star denied.

Another line of defence is 'fair comment'. This is your claim to the right to express your opinions openly and is the basis of the right to free speech. In any area which can be shown to be of legitimate public concern you may claim the right to express your views, even to the point of vulgar abuse. If you are in the public eye as politician, performing artist, company director, entertainer, official or spokesman your activities are liable to comment. What is not permissible is to use comment to disseminate factual libels. Opinion based upon, or implying, erroneous facts are libellous. If you are challenged over strongly expressed opinions you need only show that you are airing honestly held convictions. On this basis you should be able to criticize the beliefs and actions of others without fear of being sued.

However you must be shown to be free of the taint of malice. The moment your words are taken to impute dishonourable motives your defence evaporates. For example in the case of the football commentator quoted above, the libel lay not in the verbal abuse of the referee's decision but the suggestion that the basis of the decision was a desire to get a place in the history books. In an earlier case a famous television cook had lent his name to an advertisement for a commercial packet turkey stuffing. A review which commented that no proper cook would ever use such a stuffing led to a successful action on the grounds that the comment was a malicious attack upon the cook's probity. The cook still had to publicly confirm that he liked the product and used it in his own expensive restaurant.

The problems inherent in reporting potentially libellous remarks made in privileged conditions, which may include Parliament, the Courts and public meetings, are subject to special types of defence which concern reporters. Reference should be made to one of the standard works on the subject and editors and journalists need to be very clear about the rules. Again, the only insurance is to take prompt legal advice in cases of potential trouble.

However, there is one defence which is open to the TV Director. Most of the celebrated libel actions quoted above have been the concern of the narrow area of news and current affairs programmes. In these it must be generally assumed, or at least hoped, that those involved are aware of the dangers and have access to legal advice. But there are myriad ways in which the most unchallenging or least contentious sort of general programme might still run into problems of defamation. The only defence is innocence. The only prevention is careful homework.

It is possible to libel unintentionally. The case given in every legal textbook is that of Artemus Jones. In 1910 the *Sunday Chronicle* published a report on English visitors travelling to Dieppe for illicit fun and games. The characters were disguised by humorous names, one of which was Artemus Jones. Unfortunately Murphy's Law struck. There was a real Artemus Jones, a solicitor, and although clearly nothing to do with the characters in the report, nonetheless he successfully sued. History repeated itself in 1940 when Harold Newstead of Camberwell sued Express Newspapers for a report about 'Harold Newstead, a 30 year old Camberwell man, sent to prison for nine months for bigamy'. Unaware that there were two Harold Newsteads the paper was found guilty on the grounds that the bigamous one had not been clearly defined by his address. This, in part, accounts for the irritating journalistic habit of building extraneous detail into reports such as 'Rosie Bliggins, redheaded mother of three described as a model said from her sitting room in Gulag Buildings, Abersoch, Wales, that she denied. . . .

Under the Defamation Act 1952 it is possible to plead that the libel took place through accident and not carelessness. The Defendant must make an offer of amends usually in the form of a correction and sufficient apology published with due prominence. He must show that he intended no libel and was unaware of the circumstances in which the words might have applied to a third party or have been taken as libellous to that other person. Above all, most important for the Television Director, all reasonable care must have been exercised prior to publication.

Pictures can also be libellous. It is common practice to shoot general 'wallpaper' shots to illustrate essentially non-visual news stories. In a recent case an item on police corruption was illustrated by an exterior of a police station with a man walking through shot. The man happened to be an identifiable CID officer who successfully sued the BBC for £20 000.

The use of still pictures, either especially shot or from a picture library, can too easily and too frequently cause problems. In a town with more than one school the portrayal of the wrong exterior or children in the wrong uniform can be actionable. Head teachers have learned that an explicit or implicit attack upon the discipline or achievements of a school can be taken as a libel upon the professional reputation of the head teacher, even though no names are used.

The appearance of the wrong face with the wrong caption or story is a regular nightmare and so clearly the result of carelessness that the narrow defence of 'innocence' could hardly apply.

As Artemus Jones illustrated, the invention of personal names is no sure protection. Neither is the invention of names of products, postal addresses or telephone numbers. So the fact that your production is manifestly a work of complete fiction may not save you from considerations of libel. The way to minimize the risks is to follow the procedure known as Negative Checks.

Place names Check place names in local gazeteers and telephone directories. There may not be a Dorset village called Fidget Monachorum with a Satan worshipping vicar, but it pays to check.

Addresses If you set your piece in an identifiable town avoid using real, or potentially real, addresses. Even if your context appears quite harmless or even flattering to the occupants there are still some people who cannot resist firing off threatening, abusive or begging letters to any television address however patently concocted.

Telephone numbers Never use a permutation of telephone numbers which may be real. Avoid the temptation to make them up and dial them in vision as a last minute improvization.

Car number plates Before using a real number plate on screen make sure that the real owner has no objections to his vehicle being identified in a fictional context. If fake numbers are made, ensure that the number is not shared with any actual regulation. Remember it is illegal to use a fake numberplate on a public highway.

Brand names It is common practice for people to use trade names as portmanteau terms for commercial products. People often refer to vacuum cleaners as Hoovers, to the despair of Electrolux and a dozen other manufacturers. Photocopiers get carelessly lumped together as Xerox, ball point pens as Biros, except in France where they are Bics, most transparent adhesive tape gets called Sellotape and so on. Be careful not to show or verbally identify such products in a perjorative circumstance, or to use the wrong product name in conjunction with a rival manufacturer. If you are to portray a broken down refrigerator full of putrid food make sure you don't show any identifying logo or trade name and avoid brand names in the script.

Other names Since 1982 there has been no compulsory central registration for the names of small businesses so to avoid committing a Harold Newstead blunder any name given to a ficticious small shop or company should be checked and then unambiguously identified. It is foolish, as well as unimaginative, to go for obvious common names like Hotel Majestic or Worldwide Travel Agents as these are likely to exist in any large town. There are dozens of Grand Hotels, Church Lanes and Red Lion pubs. Less obvious areas where you can come unstuck are the names of clinics and hospitals, airport flight numbers, cinemas, theatres and the names, real or assumed, of actors and pop musicians, company directors, policemen, song titles, jockeys, journalists, ships and members of the nobility, the professions and officers in the armed forces. Most of these can be checked from obvious sources such as *Burke's Peerage*, *The Stock Exchange Yearbook*, *The Law List* or the *Medical Directory*.

Remember, it is even possible to defame a horse, or more precisely, its owner. Citing the name of a little winner in the context of a broken-down nag or a case of race fixing may lead to prosecution for malicious falsehood.

Malicious falsehood

Malicious falsehood is a separate offence from libel and one that is not heard before a jury. The prime consideration is not the protection of the reputation of the Plaintiff but to establish that the actual words used were false, that they were published through spite, dishonesty or for financial advantage, or that they caused or were likely to cause loss. Malice may not mean pure vindictiveness. A statement is malicious if it is shown that the defendant didn't care whether what he published was true or false. This would be the case with the unfairly maligned racehorse. Damage must be shown to have been likely to have occurred.

Malicious falsehood is difficult to prove but don't let that stop you taking care. Avoid sloppy reporting where someone who is hale, hearty and successfully practising his profession is referred to as 'past it'. This might land you in court.

Rehabilitation of Offenders Act

There is one specific exception to the defence of absolute truth in a defamation suit, and that is covered by the Rehabilitation of Offenders Act 1974. The law is intended to defend citizens who have a criminal record from having past convictions brought up long after the event to the ruin of their restored reputations. Convictions are regarded as 'spent' after a fixed period according to the severity of the sentence. The law only considers comparatively minor sentences. Any term of imprisonment of over two and a half years can never be 'spent'. Below that there are four fixed rehabilitation periods for adults and more detailed provisions for young offenders.

For sentences between six months and two and a half years the amnesty comes into force after ten years, and after six years for a custodial sentence of under six months. Fines or community service orders are spent after five years and for an absolute discharge the amnesty period is six months. Similar periods apply to those convicted by court-martial.

A plaintiff will claim that anyone publishing such details of spent conviction is acting from malice. It is possible that the defence of public interest might be employed if, for example, current circumstances would lead to concern, e.g. someone with an undisclosed string of minor drug or sex offences applying to run a children's home. But the defence will be on very shaky ground.

Data Protection Act

Another unusual piece of legislation which caused a flurry at the time of introduction is the Data Protection Act 1984. People have a right of access to information held about them on computer systems. If they dispute such data they may insist on having it corrected and have a right to sue for damages if the data is harmfully inaccurate or if it has been disclosed to unauthorized parties. Any organization which keeps data on living persons in a computer system has to register with the Data Protection Registrar. Failure to register is a criminal offence, as is the use of such data for purposes other than those stated at the time of registration. So people have a right to know what information is being held about them and can demand access to it within forty days of a request being made. The Registrar has powers of entry and inspection. Because of possible defamation charges journalists have been generally advised not to keep more than a minimum of information on their computers since notes taken during the preparation of a programme or journalistic investigation by their nature are likely to contain unsubstantiated reports, hearsay and a mixture of fact and fiction. The journalist's notebook is, then, alive and well.

A similar problem has been envisaged in storing hitherto unpublished material, such as obituaries, on computer files since these are frequently of a nature which could be seen as defamatory if published during the subject's lifetime. For all the emphasis on journalistic problems it could be overlooked that producers, agents, casting directors and many more are using the computer database. The sort of personal *aide memoire* which might have once been appended to a confidential file would make the author highly vulnerable if stored in a computer. So you are well advised not to include on the computerized records of freelance contributors or technicians, for example, remarks such as 'talentless and unreliable' or 'not to be used, normally drunk by midday.'

Secrets, sources and confidentiality

Journalists and programme makers in the topical and documentary areas cannot work without sources of information. Information is often given or has originally been received in confidence. There may be no law of privacy in England but the law of confidence has been described by Tom Crone in *Law and the Media* as a 'boom area'. Often this is thought of as an area of specific exclusive interest to news reporters getting 'off the record' tip-offs but this is not necessarily so. The use of breach of confidence is spreading to include areas of finance, industry, employment and even entertainment.

In 1981 a writer successfully proved an exception to the old television adage that there is no copyright on ideas. He was successfully able to show that he had given Thames Television an idea for a musical series in confidence and that when the company produced an almost identical product called *Rock Follies*, without employing the writer, they had acted in breach of confidence.

A more familiar textbook example was that of Schering Chemicals vs Falkman in 1981. A television producer who also worked as a training consultant became interested in a controversy surrounding the drug Primados which possibly caused damage to unborn babies. Thames Television took up the story and the facts were researched from publicly available sources. However Schering Chemicals successfully sought an injunction to have the programme suppressed on the grounds that the producer had obtained the original idea whilst in their pay and thus had broken his agreement to confidentiality. Even if there is no written contract the courts may assume a degree of confidence exists between employer and employee. In 1987 the television presenter Anne Diamond successfully sought an injunction to stop *The Sun* newspaper from publishing a front page story about her domestic life on the grounds that the information was leaked by her ex-nanny who had broken confidence. The use of an injunction, in this case delivered whilst the presses were rolling, can be a devastating blow for a newspaper and to a lesser extent a topical television show, whether the injunction is upheld by the courts later or not. Robert Maxwell appears twice in textbook contexts for using this weapon. In 1982 the *Watford Observer* planned to reveal that Sun Printers, an important local employer, was losing money and that redundancies were due. The information came through union negotiations taking place at the plant. Maxwell maintained such discussions were confidential and arranged for an injunction to be delivered at the moment when the presses were due to turn. Fortunately the paper had prepared alternative pages and the injunction was not totally ruinous. The subsequent appeal was in favour of the *Watford Observer* which nonetheless was left with a sizeable legal bill. In 1990 Maxwell was faced with two biographies, one sycophantic, the other critical. He tried unsuccessfully to issue injunctions against the publishers and booksellers on the grounds that material had been supplied to the less flattering biographer by one of his secretaries.

The use of material obtained in confidence puts the programme maker at greater risk than an injunction to stop publication or broadcast. The courts may in addition rule that the parties concerned reveal the sources of their information. In 1989 a company obtained an injunction against the trade magazine *The Engineer* and a reporter. The reporter had received a confidential report outlining financial difficulties and attempts to raise a bank loan by the company. He telephoned the company to check his information and was met not only by an injunction but a court order requiring him to disclose the name of his informant. As this was a clash of two confidences, i.e. that of the source with his employer and that of the source and a journalist, he refused to comply and was fined £5,000.

But the growth area in breach of confidence which has caused most concern during the 1980s has been its deployment by the Government to silence or punish critics as an alternative to deploying the Official Secrets Act. Whereas prosecutions under the Official Secrets Act take place before a jury which may be not at all sympathetic to the Government, a civil action for breach of confidence is not. It was only in 1975 that the idea that confidentiality could extend from private arrangements to 'public secrets' came about. The issue then was an unsuccessful attempt by the Attorney General to stop the publication of the cabinet diaries of the ex-minister Richard Crossman.

In the 1980s a revival of the concept gave rise to two *causes célèbres*, the Zircon Affair and the Spycatcher Affair. They are inter-related. The Spycatcher affair began in 1985 when Peter Wright, a former British Secret Service Officer living in Australia, proposed to publish a book of memoirs which included allegations of plots by MI5 to destabilize the Labour government of Harold Wilson. The British Attorney General unsuccessfully sought an injunction on the grounds that public security officers had lifetime obligations of confidentiality.

Almost four years of political and judicial high farce followed. The book was published, banned, serialized, printed in Ireland, smuggled into England in bulk and ultimately wearily accepted by the Court of Appeal on the grounds that 'the cat was out of the bag'. In the meantime the enraged Government lashed out at any other suspected breaches of confidence by ex-employees.

In 1987 an injunction was sought against BBC Radio 4 to stop it broadcasting a programme on the role of the security services and either naming any such past officers or using any information whatsoever supplied by them. Then came an attempt to prevent the use of material, already published, called *Inside Intelligence*, by an ex-MI6 Officer. As with *Spycatcher* different courts responded differently. The English courts upheld the Government, the Scottish ones did not.

In the same year the Government resorted to the sledgehammer of the Official Secrets Act to prevent the transmission of a BBC Scotland series called *The Secret Society* which alleged that Parliament had been deceived about the expenditure of five hundred million pounds on a secret spy satellite called Zircon. Police raided the home of the programme maker

Duncan Campbell, and the offices of *New Statesman* which intended to print the substance of the allegations. Detectives in Scotland used a warrant under the Official Secrets Act to raid BBC Scotland and take away the programme files. Campbell was ordered to hand over any documents obtained from ex-employees of the signals intelligence centre at Cheltenham GCHQ and to name his sources.

The obsession with secrecy has led to demand from both inside and outside Parliament for a complete reform of the law dealing with Official Secrets, a new Bill of Rights, and even a Freedom of Information Act similar to that which exists in the United States. Despite ministerial promises in 1992 to sweep away 'the cobwebs of secrecy' it just seems that this amounts to the right to publish the names of the heads of Security Departments and a promise to get rid of specific secrecy clauses attached to various bits of legislation. The main change has been the passing of a new version of the Official Secrets Act, which became effective in March 1990. Time will only show whether this represents a liberalization of the previous 1911 Act when it is tested before the Courts.

The Act applies only to classes of information covered by Security and Intelligence, Defence, International Relations, Crime, Government phonetapping and interception of letters and other communications, and confidential information entrusted in confidence to other states and international organizations. It is an offence for anyone to disclose unauthorized information in these categories whether it is received at first or second hand. In most, but not all cases, the prosecution will have to prove that the revelation of official secrets was actually harmful to the security of the state.

D Notices

Governments and ministries have generally used more subtle means to control what may or not be printed mainly by placing subtle pressure on companies and editors through the granting or withdrawal of facilities, the granting of access to officially inspired leaks of information for a chosen few, and general news manipulation. A long standing informal control of sensitive information is through the D notice system. D (which may stand for Defence though nobody is sure) notices are issued by the Defence Press and Broadcasting Committee which comprises on one side appointees of the Foreign Office, the Home Office and the Ministry of Defence, and on the other side representatives of the press and the broadcasting organizations. Day-to-day business is conducted by a chairman appointed from the media ranks and the permanent secretary of the Committee who is the civil servant in charge of D notices. The notices themselves are letters circulated by the D Notice secretary to news editors requesting that no details of specified areas be published or broadcast without seeking advice. The committee has no statutory powers to enforce D notices and an editor may always decide to publish and be damned. Unfortunately the lack of an objection from the Committee does not legally sanction publication and prosecution could still follow, though not probably under the Official Secrets Act. The injunction in 1987 against the BBC Radio Programme *My Country Right or Wrong* was on grounds of breach of confidence despite the programme content being passed by the D Notice Committee. In fact the general relationship between the press and the D Notice secretary has generally been amiable with a certain amount of latitude being given by the secretary over some sensitive publications. A list of D Notice subjects which range from information about nuclear weapons to the publication of photographs of Ministry of Defence property is available to the public as well as journalists.

Ireland

The law in Northern Ireland is different to that of England, Scotland, the Channel Islands and the Isle of Man. The comments made elsewhere in this book refer only to English Law.

The most important difference at present in Northern Ireland is the application of the Prevention of Terrorism Act. For example the Police and Criminal Evidence Act does not apply in Northern Ireland. Police were able in 1988 to oblige the BBC to hand over untransmitted footage of an IRA funeral using the Prevention of Terrorism Act. In Irish law it is an offence *not* to hand evidence pertaining to a criminal offence to the police. But the most important restriction was a Notice issued by the Home Secretary in October 1988 to the BBC and the IBA banning the broadcast of any expressions of support for a number of listed paramilitary groups and political organizations known to support them. The intention was to deny the terrorists 'the oxygen of publicity' by silencing both those who represented the Northern Ireland organizations named and anyone speaking out in their favour whether in the United Kingdom or elsewhere.

It is not permissible to broadcast a statement or interview with a designated terrorist supporter or a speech in support of a paramilitary group by, for example, a pro-Republican Army American congressman. However, it is allowed that such words can be set in reported speech and that pictures of interviews can be shown so long as the actual direct speech is suppressed. The same applies to events. Footage of a demonstration would be admissible but any anti-British slogans have to be wiped off the sound track. The only exceptions are speeches given in the British Parliament or by candidates at the time of a General election. Speeches in the European Parliament are not exempted. The Order was widely regarded as a serious infringement of free speech and has been challenged in the European courts. It was also seen as an example of governmental media-bashing.

What has emerged is a quintessentially Irish solution to the problem.

When an interview with a paramilitary spokesman has been shot the words are meticulously copied and the original soundtrack then wiped. Next an actor who can do an expert impersonation of the interviewee is contracted to record the original words synchronizing with the lip movements, thus restoring the item to its nearly identical original form.

As the Irish farmer said to the lost traveller 'If I was you I wouldn't have started from here in the first place'.

Contempt

The subject of Contempt of Court is of particular importance to press journalists and to television news reporters and editors.

The law exists to prevent any material published or broadcast acting in such a way as might influence the judgement of a jury or, to a lesser extent, a judge or magistrate. Contempt rules apply to any court of justice including Magistrates Courts, Courts of Appeal, Coroner's Courts, Courts Martial and even certain types of Public Enquiry and Tribunals.

There are excellent primers for journalists who are embarking on court reporting. The rules vary from court to court and can vary from offence to offence. For example there is very little indeed you may report about a juvenile offence, even after a conviction, unless the court lifts reporting restrictions. Since 1988, in rape cases you may report the personal details of the accused but may not mention or show pictures of the victim. Certain cases are heard *in camera*, others in courts from which the public have been removed but the press allowed to remain. Contempt can be very flexibly interpreted by the courts and penalties very much depend on the opinions of individual judges. A report on a national news programme might be held to be in contempt because it might have come to the notice of potential jurors. The same report transmitted on a regional programme at the other end of the country might be deemed harmless because it would not have been seen by anybody involved in the trial.

Court reporting can involve many legal niceties of which the protagonists must be constantly aware. However Murphy's Law might as easily strike at those working on programmes with little to do with daily news reporting.

A contempt is committed whether or not the perpetrator intended to influence a case and whether or not the perpetrator was aware that contempt was possible at the time. In other words you can't plead ignorance.

For a programme to be in contempt two things must have taken place. The content could be interpreted as being prejudicial to the proceedings, and the proceedings must be 'active'. A case becomes 'active' the moment that a warrant is issued, a summons served, an arrest made or someone has been charged with a crime. The case remains active until after dismissal or conviction and, to some degree, until after sentencing and the hearing of any appeal.

A case likely to involve a trial by jury will be regarded as particularly sensitive since the law assumes that juries may be easily swayed. Cases heard by judges alone, or reports made in the period between conviction and sentence, or sentence and appeal, are regarded more leniently on the assumption that judges are unlikely to take any notice of the media.

A problem for the television maker, as distinct from the newsman, is the length of time normally spent between the beginning of a project and the date of transmission. There is one highly distinguished television documentary maker who has been sitting on a completed film for a number of years. The subject is a criminous family of petty thieves. Their own participation was cheerfully given, however each time a transmission date is advertised one or other of this large clan is either on the run, on bail, on remand, in jail and appealing against sentence or similarly involved in active proceedings.

The same problem can arise when you wish to follow the process of a case with a view to completing the project immediately after a verdict. Even if you are dramatizing or partly fictionalizing the events, a late appeal can still throw a legal spanner in the works, and appeals often take a long time to come up.

However, there are exceptions. The police may waive restrictions on the basis of setting up a public hue and cry after particular crimes. Where public participation is sought to help track down a criminal, photographs or photofit impressions may be issued and detailed descriptions of a crime and suspect given. There are long running programmes of the *Crimewatch* and *Police Five* stable which depend upon such police appeals for public participation. But extreme caution still has to be exercised. A reconstruction of a crime is only an impression based on witness evidence later to be presented to the courts. You must in no way pre-empt the issue by implying that any of your performers in any way represents any of the accused. An armed raid on a security convoy at night by a gang in balaclava helmets might be filmed with dramatic panache but give little away. A case of fraud is best illustrated with shots of anonymous hands stuffing banknotes into a case or playing with a computer terminal. Even where an actual getaway car is found the number plates must be obscured since the identification of a specific vehicle by a witness might be a crucial element in the case. Of course the moment an arrest has been made the restrictions apply in full until after a conviction or a verdict of 'not guilty'.

Of course, at the end of appeals procedures a campaigning producer can in effect challenge the courts by documentary or dramatic reconstructions which imply that a miscarriage has taken place, and the early 1990s has seen a series of convictions mainly involving terrorist offences, overturned and coroners verdicts challenged. Sometimes, as with the television programme, *Who Bombed Birmingham?* cases have been re-opened and convictions quashed as a direct consequence of such media pressure.

In the courtroom

Whilst a court is in session there are strict rules about what you may or may not do in either the courtroom or the court precincts. The definition of 'court precincts' is somewhat blurred. These appear to include the interior of the courts, the steps outside and even the pavement opposite – in fact wherever a court official deems appropriate. On the other hand it would seem to be against the letter of the law to wait at the entrance of a court to get pictures of the accused or witnesses arriving and leaving, and yet this commonly occurs without a charge of contempt. It is assumed that if a warrant for arrest is issued but no arrest has been made within twelve months, often because the accused has skipped the country, then a case is no longer active and you may report on the accused in as prejudicial a way as you please. The case of Lord Lucan who has been missing since the murder of the family nanny in 1975 has been the subject of speculation and satire ever since. As a television programme maker you are more handicapped than your colleagues in the press. You may not take a camera or tape recorder into a courtroom. If you try it will, at least, be confiscated. You may be allowed to do a little discreet sketching but you may not publish such sketches. Strictly speaking, all you may do is publish sketches done from memory outside the court. You are therefore limited to a verbal summary of the bare bones of a case which includes the names of the justices and counsel, the defendants and witnesses with their occupations and addresses, although even the latter are sometimes restricted, the charges made, details of legal aid, the nature of any reporting restrictions, and, in the case of the lower courts, any details of bail or commital proceedings.

In the magistrates courts you may report a case only after it has been tried summarily or dismissed. If the magistrates commit the case for trial at a higher court you remain restricted. You certainly may not mention any wrangling in court over bail which often involves an assumption that the accused will either do a flit or re-offend before his case comes up.

During an actual trial you should restrict yourself to quotations from the words of the parties concerned and, even then, the court must be sure that such words are fair and accurate. In other words if you quote the counsel for the prosecution at his wittiest, but fail to do justice to the painstaking cross-examination by the counsel for the defence which undermines the prosecution case, you may be found to be in contempt. On the other hand if the balance of your report is fair, if all comments are fully attributed, and evidence is always represented as part of an ongoing legal argument and not established fact, you can benefit. You may enjoy the absolute privilege of reporting remarks which would be clearly libellous if reported from outside a courtroom.

You will not be allowed to shoot inside a courtroom whether or not it is in use. For courtroom scenes you must build a set or find an appropriate location. There are districts such as Oxford where old de-commissioned courtrooms have been preserved and are frequently used by film and television companies.

If you get involved in any kind of shooting in or around any kind of court do your homework, check with the court officials, and have access to a good lawyer.

Postscript

There are many subject areas left unmentioned where the director or producer may get himself into another fine mess. Perhaps a later edition will have to make room for a lengthy look at the problems of accepting programme commissions and negotiating fees.

Television production is currently very much a buyers' market with the broadcast companies shedding skilled staff by the thousand onto the freelance market. In the broadcast sector the revenue cake is being cut into more and thinner slices and budgets squeezed remorselessly. In the corporate and training sectors clients and sponsors are slashing their investment and there is no lack of unscrupulous businessmen willing to concoct shady deals in place of straight payment to tempt the hard pressed small company.

As the broadcasters turn to publishing the larger independents may become very large indeed and many of the smaller ones go to the wall, get swallowed up or leave the world of broadcasting. The BBC will be under renewed assault to embrace overt sponsorship, subscription or commercial advertising. It may be increasingly forced into bed with its arch antagonist, the satellite broadcaster. As the terrestrial and satellite channels compete for revenue and the outlets for television commercials multiply so budgets for production will be cut. The age of the wildly expensive but beautifully crafted British television commercial may be over.

Very soon, it is intended that the ITC companies will be made open to takeover bids. The big corporate predators are already getting ready. The quality of the product is not likely to be their prime concern. If the examples of France and Italy are followed any further deregularization will lead first to a collapse in the much vaunted quality of British television followed by a cut-throat pursuit of audience numbers at any price and may even result in entire broadcast channels going under.

Satellite broadcasting will become increasingly international. America's CNN and the BBC's World News (now increasingly referred to as WSTV) have shown the way. Soon the television airwaves may be as open as those of radio. As Europe moves towards some sort of federalization the old days of television as a collection of exclusive national monopolies will inevitably end. Media moguls will buy up channels to establish continent wide television giants. The widely deplored degradation of much of the British press by media tycoons does not set a happy precedent. The same tycoons may soon be free to take over TV stations.

Technology continues to run ahead of the game regardless, even though yesterday's gadgets slump in price or become obsolete and new toys of ever increasing complexity and cost are launched. Perhaps the taste for ever newer whizzbangs and effects is becoming sated but in some sectors, like promotional music videotapes, the clients still crave the latest and flashiest that digital technology can provide. Even before many broadcast companies have upgraded their video standard from one inch tape to Beta SP, there has arisen a plethora of competing and generally incompatible digital formats. There are now as many as nine available vt formats, nearly all mutually incompatible. As from 1993, all national BBC programmes apart from news and current affairs should be transmitted on the Panasonic D3 format, whilst from 1994 Channel 4 will expect delivery of programmes on Panasonic D5. Meanwhile, many of the ITV companies have plumped for the D2 format! Not surprisingly, many of the facility houses have been having a hard time.

Technological advance is uneven. The biggest game to play for is high definition television. Competing, and incompatible, systems are already in existence in Europe, Japan and America. The progress of satellite transmissions will stall until transmission standards are agreed. But even if high definition transmission were to begin tomorrow it would benefit few. High definition demands a wide screen format. The studio cameras exist and are already in use for commercials productions in particular. But the current generation of domestic high definition receivers are wildly expensive, the size of dishwashers and still not capable of doing justice to the quality of the images being transmitted. Work is going on to provide slim screens using new techniques like liquid crystals. On the other hand if high definition does overcome its problems and really takes off, then the old almost square screen and its poor 625 line resolution will be laughably old-fashioned in no time. Sets which are wide screen but not high definition are already available. The effect will inevitably knock on down the line to the most modest educational video. The new will drive out the old as surely as colour drove out monochrome twenty-five years ago. The only technology which remains future-proof is film which even now in a super-sixteen millimetre format produces a resolution of images as good as current high definition television can transmit. It would be ironic if the decade of frantically developing videotape techniques ended in a renaissance of the 'tried and tested' technology of film. If this is not to be the case, how many production companies will be able to afford the enormous costs of totally re-equipping?

Even the law is subject to repeated surprises. A very recent example has been the attempt by the Home Office to use copyright laws to sue a television company for transmitting an interview with the imprisoned murderer Denis Nilsen after an injunction had been refused by the courts. Uproar over the publication of intimate pictures and recordings of the Royal Family seem likely to prompt punitive new legal restrictions. Even the Prime Minister has taken to litigation.

Any and all of these changes will inevitably bring ever more brilliant openings for Murphy and his own unbending law. In consideration of which the fledgling director or producer might well conclude that television in the 1990s is no longer a fit occupation for a lady or gentleman and go into gardening instead. Before doing so it should be remembered that Murphy's Law does have a coda. It reads: 'there is never anything so unlikely as the inevitable'.

Appendix

Contacts, Addresses and Further Reading

When you need to take matters beyond the areas covered in this short handbook the golden rule is find out who is more knowledgeable than yourself and ask their advice. Such is the complexity of the process of making film and television that nobody is going to have all the answers. Never think that any question is too stupid. Advice is often contradictory and the goalposts seem perpetually on the move. There is nothing like experience. If you are lucky and work surrounded by good experienced producers and technicians you will find as much enlightenment in their anecdotes as in a shelf load of books and memoranda.

But remember folklore has to be taken with a pinch of salt. One year's coup can be next year's prosecution. Still not for nothing was it claimed during several decades that the collective wisdom of British television resided in the bar of the BBC Club. The following are suggestions as to where you might turn for current further enlightenment.

Chapter 1 On location

By definition locations raise purely local problems. Your most important contacts will be local officials and landowners and the managers or proprietors of commercial premises.

There are professional location finders, many regionally based. They advertise in various media trade journals or publications such as *The Broadcast Production Guide* published by International Thomson, *The International Film and Television Yearbook* published by Screen International and *British Film Institute Film and Television Handbook*.

The BBC has begun to throw open its unrivalled facilities to outsiders. Help may be requested from The Manager, Television Locations, Television Centre, Wood Lane, London W12 7RJ.

An invaluable guide to location contacts, as well as research resources in almost every area is *The Television Researcher's Guide* by Kathy Chater published by BBC Television Training.

The most comprehensive and up to date list of contacts across the industry is to be found in *The Knowledge*, obtainable from Benns Business Information Services, PO 20, Tonbridge, Kent TN9 1RQ.

For historic locations an invaluable contact is The National Trust for England and Wales who are best approached through the various regional offices to be found in the local telephone directories.

Monuments and locations financed by the Department of the Environment are listed by English Heritage, 23 Saville Row, London W1X 1AB.

Many privately owned premises may be contacted through The Historic Houses Association, 2 Chester Street, London SW1 7BB. Scotland has its own equivalent institutions.

The unenviable job of keeping an eye on things during a location shoot, and apologizing for mistakes afterwards, has often been landed on the director's PA. For further insight read *The Television PA's Handbook* by Avril Rowlands published by Focal Press and *The Production Assistant's Survival Guide* by Cathy Fraser published by BBC Television Training.

The job of location finding and administration for dramatic productions is increasingly the job of a full time location manager or production manager. A Guild of Location Managers has recently been set up with the slogan 'Somebody's Got To Do It'. Watch the trade press for developments.

The work of the Production Manager is covered in *Production Management for Film and Video* by Richard Gates, published by Focal Press.

Chapter 2 Out and About

For information and clearances for flying write to The Civil Aviation Authority, General Aviation Section, 129 Kingsway, London WC2B 6TE or The General Manager Scottish Aerodromes, The Civil Aviation Authority, Broomhill Drive, Edinburgh EH11 3XE.

Advice on private pilots and airfields can be obtained from The Aircraft Owners and Pilots' Association, 50 Cambridge St, London SW1.

Permission to shoot on or around most navigable inland waterways must be sought from The British Waterways Board, Graycaine Road, Watford, Herts WD2 4JR.

Most tidal estuarine waters and some navigable rivers, like the Thames, are subject to their own port or river authorities. There is no general right of navigation or access to waterways in England and Wales and individual landowners must be approached where appropriate. Coastguards, harbourmasters, lighthouse keepers and metereological offices should be approached locally in the first instance.

Chapter 3 Going foreign

Up-to-date information about national and airline vaccination regulations should be available from The Department of Health and Social Security, International Relations (Health) Branch, London SE1 6BY.

The Medical Advisory Service to Visitors Abroad now has clinics in most parts of the country. For your nearest centre ask a reputable travel agent or contact British Airways Travel Clinics, 7 Bury Place, London WC1A 2LA (Phone 071 831 3266).

Visa requirements are so subject to the ups and downs of international politics that it is always best to check with the consulates of the countries concerned close to the intended departure date. An agency which will undertake to help obtain visas and advise on work permits is The Visa Shop, Charing Cross Shopping Arcade, London WC2.

Chapter 4 Cast, crews and other animals

The annually revised encyclopaedia of British actors and actresses is *Spotlight* available from 32 Cranbourne Street, London WC2H 7AP.

The trade union representing actors is British Actors' Equity, 42 Cranbourne Street, London WC2H 7AP. Equity holds the registry of qualified stuntmen.

For a simple guide to the choreography and staging of action sequences read *After Tea We'll Do The Fight* by Mike Crisp published by BBC Television Training.

Special effects, and their attendant risks, are described in *Creating Special Effects for Television and Video* and *The Technique of Special Effects in Television*, both by Bernard Wilkie and published by Focal Press.

For a description of the commonest drama effects used on British television see *Does The Horse Explode? Special Effects In Television* by Peter Jarvis. BBC Television Training Publications.

The register of special effects technicians is available from Broadcasting, Entertainment and Cinematograph Technicians, 111 Wardour Street, London W1V 4AY.

Further advice and information on visual effects specialists not necessarily on the BECTU register is available from The Head of Visual Effects, BBC TV, 250 Western Avenue, London W3 6XJ.

The leading suppliers of weapons in London are Bapty's, 703 Harrow Road, London N10.

There are numbers of other specialist firms who advertise in the classified advertisement sections of the trade press and arms dealers with television or film experience may be located through the yellow pages of the telephone directory.

BBC Television has an armourer's department and stocks of weapons. They will supply both advice and materials. Contact The BBC Armourer, 355 Scenery Block, Television Centre, Wood Lane, London W12 8QT.

The standard works on military firearms, large and small, are published by Jane's Publishing Company Ltd, 238 City Road, London EC1V 2PU.

As one might expect there is no end to the list of bodies dedicated to the fancy or protection of different types of animals in Britain. The main points of reference are The Royal Society For the Protection of Cruelty To Animals, Causeway, Horsham, West Sussex RH12 1HG and The Royal Society for The Protection Of Birds, The Lodge, Sandy, Bedford SG19 2DL.

Up to date information on endangered species is published in *The Red Data Book* published by the International Union for the Conservation of Nature.

Suppliers of trained animals advertise in the usual publications.

Chapter 5 Health and safety

It is the duty of every employer under the Health and Safety at Work Act to draw up and publish its own regulations. Unfortunately the application of the Act to individual circumstances can be subject to wide variation of interpretation. You may find that, for example, the Health and Safety rules in two adjacent hospitals may be at variance and even contradictory. For full information contact The Health and Safety Executive, Chepstow Place, Westbourne Grove, London W2 4TF.

Note that if you have a company regularly employing more than five people you have a legal obligation to draw up your own health and safety schedule and submit this to the Executive. Names of insurance companies specializing in film and television are advertised in the publications suggested for Chapter 1.

Chapter 6 Copyright

The main reference work is *Blackstone's Guide to the Copyright, Designs and Patents Act 1988* which includes a very readable analysis and the complete text of the Act.

Each of the main copyright protection agencies and professional organizations has issued some sort of summary and commentary for its own members. Amongst the most useful are *Visual Arts and Crafts Guide to The New Laws of Copyright and Moral Rights* by Henry Lydiate published by Brittania Publications and obtainable from the Design and Artists Copyright Society, DACS, 2 Whitechurch Lane, London E1 7QR, *Rights Clearances* edited by Deborah Wolfson, published by the Association of Independent Producers, *The Photographers' Guide to the 1988 Copyright Act* obtainable from the British Photographers' Liaison Committee, 9 Domingo Street, London EC1 0TA.

Advice on script copyright is available to members through the Writers' Guild of Great Britain, 430 Edgeware Road, London W2 1EH.

Independent producers are advised to join either the International Visual Communications Association, 5 Clipstone Street, London W1P 7EP which represents mainly the non-broadcast sector or the Producers' Alliance for Cinema and Television (PACT) at Gordon House, Greencoat Place, London SW1 1PH which covers the broadcasting independents.

Both organizations have a range of publications to update their members on changes in copyright, as well as an enormous range of other topics.

Information on picture and photographic collections may be found in *The Picture Researcher's Handbook*, by Hilary and Mary Evans published by the Mary Evans Picture Library.

Up-to-date information of collections is available from The British Association of Picture Libraries and Agencies, 13 Woodberry Crescent, London N10 1PJ.

To track down copyright on feature films an essential first stop is *Halliwell's Film Guide* published by Granada Publishing Ltd. This will give the main original credits for most English language movies. The best up-to-date source of information is the British Film Institute Film and Video Library, 21 Stephen Street, London W1, who may also be able to clear rights for a limited number of productions. They also have a large stills library and will provide prints cheaply. Note though that film stills are often treated for copyright purposes as integral with the movie and so are subject to movie copyright clearances.

There are commercial copyright clearance agencies who advertise in trade publications. Two are The Clip Shop, 47 Dean Street, London W1V 5HL and Film Research and Production Services, 25 Heddon Street, London W1R 7LG.

Lists and addresses of main distributors and film collections and libraries are available from most yearbooks or through the relevant professional associations. Also see Kathy Chater's *The Television Researchers Guide* and *Researchers Guide to British Film and Television Collections* from the British Universities Film and Video Council, 55 Greek Street, London W1V 5LR.

Advice on video productions can be obtained from the British Video Association, 22 Poland Street, London W1V 3DD.

Chapter 7 Music and musicians

The main organization representing musicians is the Musicians Union (MU) 60 Clapham Road, London W2 1EH from whom an up-to-date summary of agreements and rate card for independent film and television production can be obtained.

The main copyright protection organizations are The Mechanical Copyright Protection Society Limited (MCPS), 41 Streatham High Road, London SW16 1ER, The Performing Rights Society Ltd, 29/33 Berners Street, London W1P 4AA, and The Music Publishers' Association (MPA), 103 Kingsway, London WC2B 6QX.

Record companies are represented by the British Phonographic Industry (BPI), 283–287 Regent Street, London W1R 7PB.

To sort out problems of copyright clearance in the United States begin with The American Society of Composers Authors and Publishers (ASCAP), Suite 10, 52 Haymarket, London SW1Y 4RP.

London Weekend Television offers a service to handle music copyright enquiries and negotiations for anything from feature films to corporate videos. Write to LWT Music Services, Younger's Building, Upper Ground, London SE1 9LT.

Chapter 8 Blasphemy, race, sedition and sex

For problems with the courts see the legal works suggested below.

The main regulatory bodies are The Advertising Standards Authority, 2–16 Torrington Place, London WC1E 7HN, The British Board of Film Classification, 3 Soho Square, London W1V 5DE, Broadcasting Complaints Commission, 35 Grosvenor Gardens, London SW1W 0BS, Broadcasting Standards Council, 5 The Sanctuary, London SW1P 3JS, The Independent Television Commission, 70 Brompton Road, London SW3 1EY (which will be moving to 33 Foley Street, London W1P 7LB in the summer of 1993).

Chapter 9 Defamation, contempt and other legal problems

The standard work on legal pitfalls in the media is *Media Law* by Robertson and Nicol, published by Longman. More concise and readable handbooks are *Law and the Media* by Tom Crone from Butterworth-Heinemann and McNae's *Essential Law for Journalists* from Butterworth Law Publishers.

The Defence, Press and Broadcasting Committee (D Notices) is at Room 2235, Ministry of Defence, Main Building, Whitehall, London SW1A 2HB.

Those most likely to fall foul of the law are journalists who are represented by The National Union of Journalists, 314 Gray's Inn Road, London WC1X 8DP.

Non-active telephone numbers may be obtainable from British Telecom, Numbers Allocations, 151 Shaftesbury Avenue, London WC2 HBA.

Fictitious car registration numbers are supplied by The Driving and Vehicle Licensing Centre, Swansea SA99 1AB.

Limited Companies are listed on a database kept at The Companies Registration Office, 55 City Road, London EC1.

For a fee trade names and marks may be checked through Trade Marks Registry, 66–71 High Holborn, London WC1R 4TP.

The most comprehensive collection of data for negative checking and a professional research service is BBC Data Services, Henry Wood House, Langham House, London W1A 1AA.

Index